PRAYER
between
FRIENDS

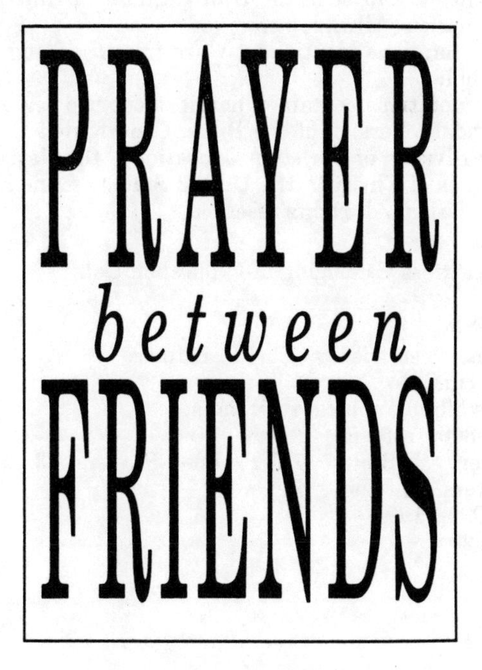

EARL F. PALMER

Fleming H. Revell Company
Tarrytown, New York

Unless otherwise identified, Scripture quotations contained herein are from the New Revised Standard Version of the Bible, copyrighted, 1989 by the Division of Christian Education of the National Council of the Churches of Christ in the United States of America, and are used by permission. All rights reserved.

Scripture quotations identified KJV are from the King James Version of the Bible.

Scripture quotations contained herein identified RSV are from the Revised Standard Version of the Bible, Copyrighted © 1946, 1952, 1971, by the Division of Christian Education of the National Council of the Churches of Christ in the United States of America, and are used by permission. All rights reserved.

Library of Congress Cataloging-in-Publication Data

Palmer, Earl F.
Prayer between friends / Earl F. Palmer.
p. cm.
Includes bibliographical references.
ISBN 0-8007-1655-8
1. Prayer. 2. Bible. O.T. Psalms—Prayers. 3. Bible. O.T. Job—Prayers. 4. Lord's prayer. I. Title.
BV210.2.P23 1991
242'.2—dc20 91-21869
CIP

Published by the Fleming H. Revell Company
Tarrytown, New York 10591
Printed in the United States of America

TO
the Wednesday-morning prayer group:

Bob, Wilbur, Blondie, Roger, Allen, Henry,
Russell, Steve, Darrell, Francois, Al, Minor,
Ted, Bill, Richard, Lou, Mark, John, Kurt,
Rene, Jan, Dick, Jim, Russ, Bob, and Walter

Contents

Part III: Praying in Jesus' Name

Preface

Prayer is a lifelong part of the Christian life. The youngest children know how to do it, because prayer is easy to learn. When we are old, we seek God even more, because our experiences with the Lord of time have enriched the meaning of prayer.

We pray when we need help, when we grieve, when we rejoice; we pray when we are afraid, and when we are thankful. Like our relationships with people, our prayers journey with us throughout all of our life, and they become inseparable from the history of that journey.

I hope that the Old Testament and New Testament explorations in these pages will focus our minds and steady our hearts so that we may pray knowing the One who invites not only our prayers but our friendship.

I am grateful to God for people in my own life who have taught me the meanings and the experiences of prayer: Ralph Byron, Persis Sueltz, Henrietta Mears, Thelma

Enkema, Bill Brown, Helen Vaughn, Eunice and Henry Gertmanian, Vera Kerr, Cathie Nicoll, and Kay MacDonald; my family, Shirley, Anne, Jon, and Elizabeth; and especially, three prayer groups in my life—the Original Twelve at Princeton, the Monday pastor's support group, and the Wednesday-morning group.

Introduction

I am convinced that, just like friendship, prayer is for amateurs. A friendship is not a professional skill in which a college gives degrees and certificates; prayer shares the same informal and nontechnical nature.

Friendship has ceremonial events, like the time when a close friend asks another to stand at a marriage ceremony as best man, maid of honor, or an attendant. But these formal occasions only happen because at a very personal level a profound unity of acknowledgment and shared joy already exists between the two people.

The Bible describes the formal acknowledgment of friendship between God and people as a covenant or promise; fundamentally that relationship really has nothing to do with ceremony, though ceremonies and public events may be used to make the promise visible or may be celebrated to honor the existence of the covenant.

The friendship already exists by the time the ceremony takes place.

Prayer is the language of that friendship with God, and my goal in this book is for us to dialogue on the meanings of prayer as that language. Within the journey of faith, people of all ages and of every kind of theological opinion feel concerned about the meanings of prayer. Because friendship with Almighty God involves a mystery and a profound wonder of grace, these concerns are often quite complicated.

Some of the most painful human experiences have to do with personal loneliness, and these concerns have at their core, I believe, a yearning for friendship with God. We ask, "How can I know that God really cares about my life when I don't feel the presence of his love?" In very practical terms spiritual loneliness must finally focus upon the possibility and reality of prayer so that we have permission to go to God with our deepest feelings.

Questions about prayer come up almost every day, in one way or another, especially from students in the university city where I serve as a pastor. I am often asked, "How can I know what God's will is for my life?" This is at least 50 percent a question about prayer. Others ask related questions, like, "Do I need to go to church to know God?" A variety of queries sooner or later become questions about prayer.

Many people find *prayer* a confusing word and idea. For some it is primarily a religious procedure that they must surround by the careful trappings of a formal religious setting. But I don't agree at all with this type of limitation. Most certainly we wouldn't let this kind of thinking affect our relationships with other people, yet for some strange reason many of us at times depend on religious practices to characterize our friendship with God.

Others view prayer as a means of power and authority. They see prayer as a religious transaction involving requests made of God. Consequently, these folk see prayer as a skill to be learned and mastered. Their understanding produces students of the art of prayer, who attend seminars on prayer methods, as if praying were an art form in which the key element was related to *our* ability at timing and technique.

The Bible includes prayers that result from the relationship between ordinary people like us and God. We will explore the greatest mystery about prayer—the truth that prayer has more to do with God's character than with our methods and techniques. That mystery is hidden in the promise of Jesus Christ to his disciples, when he invited them and ordinary people in all of time to ask what they will in Jesus' name.

In the "in his name" instruction we discover the deepest mystery of prayer, which allows us to blurt out our concerns to the One who is our best Friend. The good news is that we need no special training in "blurting out." No rituals or ceremonies qualify us to pray. So let us now begin our quest into the meaning of our own experiences of prayer. Part of our task in this venture will be to unlearn some of our earlier misconceptions so that we become free to simply ask and experience the friendship that makes our prayers possible.

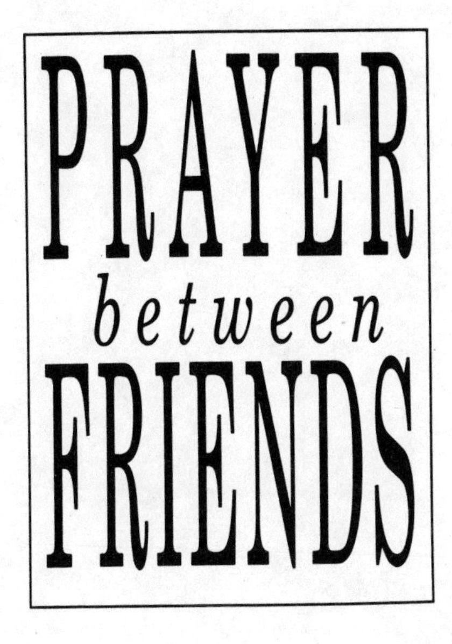
PRAYER
between
FRIENDS

Part I

Communication With Our Greatest Friend—God

1

Do I Dare Disturb God?

A student at Harvard wrote a masterful poem, telling the story of a man who wonders what his life is all about. One mark of that character's depleted sense of self-worth is his inability to pray or to even consider that his prayers matter at all. Two lines especially express his feelings: "Do I dare Disturb the universe?"[1]

Actually, the question T. S. Eliot's character expressed in "The Love Song of J. Alfred Prufrock" was also the question of the author, a young agnostic. After Eliot discovered the reality of Jesus Christ, he came to a whole new understanding of prayer. Later works, *Murder in the Cathedral* and *Journey of the Magi*, became the artistic and theological answers to the questions he asked in "Prufrock." The tentative and incomplete prayers in Eliot's first poems are replaced by a profoundly integrated whole understanding of prayer, reflected in every part of his later works.

Dare We Disturb the Universe? At some time we all ask Eliot's question about the very possibility of prayer: "Do I dare disturb?" Unambiguously, exultantly, and thoughtfully, the Bible affirms, "Yes, we can disturb the universe by our questions of the universe's Creator." But the Scripture goes even further as it proclaims that the One who created the human ear is able to hear us when we speak. The One who made us able to think, feel, care, and hope also thinks, feels, cares, and makes hope a possibility. The mystery of our freedom that enables these possibilities is united with the mystery of God's freedom. God is the ultimate source before all sources, and the ultimate wonder prior to all other wonders is that God is knowable by mere human beings. That knowability makes prayer both exciting and important.

Prayer is the word that describes our personal experience of God. As men and women who live in time and space we can know God as he makes himself known to us, and this is profound, good news. Yes, there is a relationship between us and the God who made us and who loves us.

Toward Understanding Prayer

Merely admitting that God does listen and that we need to pray does not answer all our questions concerning this glorious relationship with the Creator. A couple of incidents from my own life show forth two difficulties in our understanding of prayer.

Shortly after I graduated from theological seminary, I was assigned, as a young pastor, to speak to the youth section of a week-long conference at Mt. Hermon Christian Conference Center in California. The principal speaker during that week was Dr. Donald Grey Barnhouse, a brilliant biblical preacher and teacher, who pastored Tenth Presbyterian Church, in Philadelphia.

One afternoon, during a question-and-answer session, Dr. Barnhouse was asked, "Do you feel that our prayers change anything?"

His answer was swift and electrifying: "Our prayers only change us. They don't change God. And they don't change God's decisions about history."

Dr. Barnhouse then explained that in his opinion prayer is in its essence and totality the act of our personal submission to God's authority and of our grateful trust in the faithful love of God. He pointed out that prayer is no more than that, and to claim more on our part only shows we misunderstand the sovereign right of God over history. He asserted that God's character does not change to meet our prayer requests, nor do his decisions. We are the ones who change, and that is the good result of prayer as we bring ourselves into the presence of the Lord.

Dr. Barnhouse's tight and logical reasoning impressed me, but I still felt uneasy. The problem with his answer is that this teaching interprets the character of God—which Dr. Barnhouse saw as at the heart of Christian prayer—as rigid and immovable. It seemed to me then that this interpretation only captured part of the whole truth.

My uneasiness with the answer made me determined to look more closely at what the Bible teaches about the mystery and the meaning and the practice of prayer. Now I look back to that week with gratitude, for like a good teacher, Dr. Barnhouse had forced me to study the biblical texts that are the final authoritative source for every doctrine and promise.

Not long after this event, a challenge from almost the opposite direction confronted me. At the time I was minister to students at the University Presbyterian Church in Seattle, Washington. A fellow pastor invited me to have lunch with him, and we talked about the world crisis and the needs of youth for the gospel. I felt our discussion was being too carefully guided by my host, and the point of his careful conversation finally became clear when he asked, "Earl, do you have as much power in your life and in your prayers as you wish you had?" I answered truthfully and told my friend that I usually felt inadequate to meet the challenge of my calling.

"Earl," he asked, "do you have in your life the gifts of the Holy Spirit? Especially do you have the gifts to make prayer a power-filled experience in all of your life?" Without awaiting my answer, he told me about some of his intercessory prayer victories.

Warily I decided to answer his original questions from the standpoint of the fellowship I belonged to and was accountable to. I replied, "You should ask those who know me best to answer those questions."

Whereas Dr. Barnhouse had caused me to feel theological discomfort about the inflexibility of God's faithfulness, I now felt troubled at the prospect of the God who could be manipulated by my devoted spirituality. This emphasis on my personal experience of prayer and spirituality was too dynamic and too dependent on what was happening in me. While the idea that prayer is only our submission to the sovereignty of God seemed rigid and incomplete, in the face of the biblical witness, these lunchtime questions implicitly seemed to place too much emphasis on *my* experience.

Limiting or Attempting to Control God

These incidents typify the tensions we face as we seek to understand prayer. Dr. Barnhouse's interpretation holds the danger of limiting our understanding of God, because it contains speculative theological conclusions about the implications of God's sovereignty. This may actually create an artificial and nonbiblical boundary around prayer, which acts as a tight and final circle. Because it may give us the idea that God will not change anything as a result of our prayers, such theology downgrades the full possibilities of intercessory prayer.

My fellow pastor's portrayal of prayer moves in an opposite direction, toward arrogance or even impudence. The idea here is that our earnest prayers of agreement and requests somehow compel or even control God. Though we pray "in Jesus' name," we make both promises and demands that attempt to limit God's sovereignty as we too tightly define what we believe is the way of his love. Our assurance becomes directly related to what we describe as answers to prayer instead of simple trust in the faithful and good character of God.

Both possibilities are rooted in Christian conviction, and both need to move toward a biblical higher ground, if we are to build a healthy practice and understanding of prayer. It seems to me that what we need is to give careful attention to the promises Scripture makes to us about prayer. In looking at the biblical record, we will learn by observation how the men and women of the Bible lived and prayed. There we will find both good examples and bad, for their stories are uneven, just as ours are. Through them, though, we can learn much about God's faithfulness.

Threats to Our Understanding of Prayer

More dangerous threats to our understanding of the meaning of prayer exist than these two, which originate from within the family of believers. For example, atheism claims that human prayer has no meaning, because no ultimate Friend listens to our prayers. This claim, of course, comes from people who have not met and trusted Jesus of Nazareth. We don't need to argue the "case for prayer" with such critics. Rather, we seek to witness to them and introduce them to the Lord Jesus Christ. Only then can we appropriately press the matter further, because, in reality, prayer is a vital part of our journey of discovery as to who Jesus is.

An even more complicated threat in a sense arises from a page torn out of the book of faith, as people have misread the biblical teachings and understandings of the Bible about prayer. In their desire for spiritual and physical power, they have separated "the power from the promise." The Book of Acts describes such a man, who desired the power he witnessed in the life and actions of the early Apostles. In an effort to acquire that power, Simon attempted to buy it from Peter, saying, " 'Give me also this power so that anyone on whom I lay my hands may receive the Holy Spirit.' " Peter replied, " 'May your silver perish with you, because you thought you could obtain God's gift with money! You have no part or share in this, for your heart is not right before God' " (Acts 8:18–21).

Separation of "the power from the promise" is nothing new. The Gnostics, who opposed the apostolic gospel in the early church, attempted to acquire the power they saw in the lives of the first-century Christians. But they wanted power without obedience to the historical person and work of Jesus Christ. A Greek philosophical and mythological worldview that exalted everything that seemed "spiritual" had influenced the Gnostics, causing them to despise and reject anything physical and concrete; they were determined to arrange for a spiritual escape from the physical world. This made them highly selective about the parts of the New Testament they were prepared to embrace. Completely rejecting the Old Testament insistence upon concreteness and the inseparability of life as a whole experience of body, soul, and spirit, the Gnostic movement attempted to redesign Jesus into a spiritual force—a phantomlike Christ of spiritual power who helped religious "experts" who had the secret knowledge (gnosis) about spiritual truth, who enabled them in their goal to become fully spiritualized.

Through the centuries, movements at the edges of the Christian faith have believed and taught variations of this highly spiritualistic Gnostic theme. In fact, many theological debates in the second-century church centered on the challenge to the New Testament gospel by the Gnostic movements. A specific prayer ideology that involved the symbolic significance of certain words and ceremonies and the use of certain metals, gems, crystals, and even the importance of spiritually receptive shapes such as pyramids have characterized these movements.

Gnostic techniques sought to enable the one who mastered such special knowledge to become a channel of spiritual energy and power. Most of the Gnostic movements eventually believed and taught that deity resided in some way within personhood and was available for use and mastery if one could learn the secret methods of recovery. First-century Gnosticism resulted in self-preoccupation and an all-absorbing concentration on power.

This not-uncommon spiritual theme traces back to the

oldest, most deceptive, and pervasive promise of the tempter to Adam and Eve—spiritual and physical power stemming from secret knowledge learned by an inner and select few.

The Mystery of Prayer

Prayer, as we now see, is not so simple a matter after all. It means different things to different people. But in truth, when we think and feel together about prayer, we are thinking and feeling at the very deepest level within our personalities. The use of such a simple word as *prayer* is very important to us and to our life journeys. Consequently, in our search for truth we need to ask the really major questions and try to understand the answers as we find them.

While prayer, in a certain sense, is a very simple personal matter, it retains a profound mystery. One of my favorite lines in A. A. Milne's book *When We Were Very Young* points to this. Little Christopher Robin, human hero of the Winnie the Pooh books, is kneeling by his bed before he goes to sleep. We are told to be quiet, "Hush! Hush! Whisper who dares! Christopher Robin is saying his prayers." Why should we hush? What is so special about prayer that people whisper and tiptoe when they stumble onto someone who is praying?

Actually, prayer's mystery has little to do with our feelings about it or the methods we use. But it has everything to do with the wondrous meaning of prayer as a possibility granted to human beings by God. In the most fundamental sense, prayer is what happens when we stand as human beings at the place of agreement with God, our Friend. In other words, in our praying we lay claim to the revealed character of God. We pray not in order to catch the attention of God but because *he* has caught *our* attention. Our prayers do not create God's love for us or for those for whom we pray. Rather, we pray because the truth that God has first loved us has dawned on us.

God invites us to speak to him, and he listens when we speak. Like the hymn writer of Psalm 100:5, we claim the Lord's revealed character. He prayed confidently, because "the Lord is good; his steadfast love endures forever, and his faithfulness lasts for all generations." When we pray in Jesus' name, we make the same claim. Our prayers are not dependent upon our own earnestness or our own desperation or our own efficient use of religious language. Because of God's prior love for us, which he concretely revealed in the life and death and resurrection of Jesus Christ, our prayers have meaning. We claim that good decision of God's grace and faithfulness when we pray.

An Invitation to Friendship and Involvement

We not only claim God's grace when we pray, we also ask for things to happen—we make requests, and these, too, are a part of the mystery of prayer.

First of all God has invited us into friendship with him. Jesus was very clear about this in the promise he made to his disciples in the upper room discourse (John 13–16). Jesus firmly established the friendship factor by saying, " 'You are my friends if you do what I command you. I do not call you servants any longer, because the servant does not know what the master is doing; but I have called you friends . . .' " (John 15:14, 15).

At the same time God invites us to participate in the flow of history. What an astounding truth: Our prayers do in fact influence the course of history! Earlier in that same conversation Jesus had said, " 'Very truly, I tell you, the one who believes in me will also do the works that I do and, in fact, will do greater works than these, because I am going to the Father. *I will do whatever you ask in my name, so that the Father may be glorified in the Son. If in my name you ask me for anything, I will do it*' " (John 14:12–14, *italics mine*). All of this simply means that as friends of God we have a decisive role, through our prayers and our lives, in the events of history. Jesus does not surrender his own authority to the prayers of his disciples, but he invites them, as friends, to lay claim to that good authority.

When I reflect on the promises about prayer that Jesus gave his followers, I wonder about my own experiences of prayer in the morning, at meal times, and before I go to sleep at night. I can't help but wonder, *Are my prayers shaping history*? At the same time I wonder if I realize the profound meanings of the mystery in the divine invitation Jesus gave when he said, " 'Until now you have not asked for anything in my name. Ask and you will receive, so that your joy may be complete' " (John 16:24).

This leads me to ask, "What is your experience in prayer?" Do you have that awareness of divine appointment? Can those who observe us find themselves whispering, "Hush, this person is praying"? It seems to me that when that sense of "hush" dawns upon us, we are ready to think together about the meaning and the mystery of prayer. Let us begin our search with Bible in hand as we closely watch the ways that the people in the Bible pray. As we examine the writings in both the Old and New Testaments—specifically the Psalms, the Book of Job, and the Lord's Prayer—we will take a prayer pilgrimage. Further, our pilgrimage will come alive as we pray—as we learn by doing. For at heart, prayer is not technique or *gnosis* or theory or power. Rather, prayer is a language of relationship, and best of all, it is the language used between friends.

2

The Language of Love

At the beginning of our prayer journey, we must try to understand the ways that the language of prayer is used within the Scriptures. The Bible is our faithful guidebook for all of the questions about faith and life; it is also our guidebook to the meaning of prayer. The men and women portrayed in the Bible teach us on every page about who God is and who we are. By their own experiences they also teach us about discipleship, worship, and prayer. If we want to understand the way people feel about any subject, we must first attend to what they say; we must listen closely to the words the writers of the Bible select to express their feelings and thoughts and how they build words into sentences.

In addition to overhearing what the people of the Bible—our spiritual ancestors—say, wherever possible we also want to carefully observe what they do. How do they combine their language with their actions? When we notice this interrelationship, events and meanings come together into a whole. The Bible helps us make both of these observations because its narratives tell stories about real people and what they experienced and how they felt. As a part of its record, the Bible has also given us some of their prayers. This makes it possible for us to learn about prayer as the people of the biblical narratives do it. We learn by watching their prayers, which happen everywhere—in the temple, in a lonely cave, in private places, in joyous fellowship gatherings, and on the cross.

The Bible records at least five kinds of prayer in the Old Testament.

1. Words of Praise. Prayers of praise are called the Hallel prayers. The most famous prayer word that is used in the Old Testament is the Hebrew word *hallal*, which means "magnify, boast, shout." This is a word of excitement and joyous urgency. When "hallal" is combined with the holy name for God—"Yahweh"—it becomes the Hebrew word *hallelujah*. We find "Hallelujah" frequently in the Psalms, and it is translated in our Bibles as "Praise the Lord" (*see* Psalm 113:1). Psalms 113–118 are known as the Hallel, and Psalm 136 is the Great Hallel.

The other Hebrew words in the Old Testament praise vocabulary are not as familiar to those who speak Western languages, though each plays a key role in enabling us to understand the feelings and thoughts of men and women in the Old and New Testaments when they thought of praise. Two words closely related in mood to *hallal* are the Hebrew words *shir*, which means "sing," and *psalm*, which translates "song." Like *hallal*, these are joyous and explosive words. We see both in Psalm 137:4, "How could we sing the Lord's song in a foreign land?" *Shir* is also used in Isaiah 42:10, "Sing to the Lord a new song, his praise from the end of the earth! . . ."

2. Asking Prayer Words. Another group of prayer words in the Old Testament might be designated as the asking words. Most commonly translated "pray," they carry the sense of "ask, to request a favor."

The three major Hebrew asking words are:

a. *Atar*, which in its root form carries the idea of sacrifice. It is used in Genesis 25:21, "Isaac prayed to the Lord for his wife. . . ."
b. *Shaal* means "to ask, beg" and is used 176 times in the Old Testament. For example, in Psalm 122:6, we read, "Pray for the peace of Jerusalem. . . ."
c. *Hanan* means "to present oneself acceptably in order to ask a favor." It appears in Jeremiah 3:21: "A voice on the bare heights is heard, the plaintive weeping of Israel's children. . . ." Daniel uses it in his great prayer: " '. . . We do not present our supplications before you on the ground of our righteousness, but on the ground of your great mercies' " (9:18).

These asking words are sometimes used in a negative sense, too. *Shaal* is used that way in Psalm 78:18, "They tested God in their heart by demanding the food they craved." Believing prayer asks of God, but not all askings are prayers of faith.

3. Cries for Help. Some prayer words might be labeled "cries for help." One such powerful word is *shapak*, which means "to pour out." We find it in Lamentations 2:19, ". . . Pour out your heart like water before the presence of the Lord. . . ." We hear David use this word in Psalm 142:2, "I pour out my complaint before him. . . ."

Another "cry for help" is the Hebrew word *shaag*, which literally means "roar." This is the word used in Psalm 22:1, "My God, my God, why have you forsaken me? [Literally, "Why are you so far from the words of my roaring?"]" David also prays with this word in Psalm 38:8, "I am utterly spent and crushed; I groan [roar] because of the tumult of my heart." In both references, the translators of the Revised Standard Version use the English word "groan." But the Hebrew is more accurately translated by the stronger word "roar," the same word that is used for the roar of a lion in Old Testament texts.

The word *shava*, which means "to cry," is also part of this group of intense and deeply emotional words for prayer. Psalm 22:5 uses it, "To you they cried, and were saved. . . ."

Another word in this group, *anach*, means "to sigh." An example of its use is found in Lamentations 1:21, "They heard how I was groaning with no one to comfort me. . . ."

The most famous of these "cry for help" words is *hosanna*, which literally means "help, please." It is used in Psalm 118:25, "Save us we beseech you, O Lord! . . ." When Jesus rode into Jerusalem on that first Palm Sunday, the writer of John's Gospel tells us that the crowd cried, "Hosanna"—"Lord, help us, please."

4. "Thinking Through" Prayer Words. Our Bible also uses three words in intercessory prayer—the "thinking things through" prayers. Chief among these is *pala*, which means "to decide, assess, estimate, think through." This word is used eighty-four times in the Old Testament and represents the intercessory act of praying. English versions often translate it "intercession." It describes that intercessory thoughtfulness found in Solomon's prayer found in 1 Kings 8:28, "Regard your servant's prayer and his plea. . . ." The Prophet used *pala* to describe the Lord's house as "a house of prayer" (Isaiah 56:7).

A deliberate, sober thoughtfulness lies at the core of this word. It represents the prayer of the mind that thinks through an issue before God. The prayer of intercession may be described as an intellectual work of careful consideration of human need and divine promise before God.

Another fascinating word in this group, *haga*, means "to hum, reflect, meditate." This is the word used in Psalm 19:14, "Let the words of my mouth and the meditation of my heart be acceptable to you, O Lord, my rock and my redeemer." A related word, *maskil*, also means "to think through." This word is used as a title for several Psalms, for example "A Maskil of Asaph" (Psalm 78).

These three words point up the intellectually dynamic role of the person who prays. This kind of prayer not only shouts out in praise or cries out in distress or makes requests of God, it also decides and thinks through in order to intercede in behalf of need. This is the prayer that seeks to understand the will of God and to think through a crisis with him. These are words of partnership, "Come now, let us argue it out [reason together] says the Lord" (Isaiah 1:18).

5. Prayer Words of Obedience and Faith. Then there are the *shema* prayers, "Hear O Israel . . ." (Deuteronomy 6:4). The *shema* prayers are very important, for they express the obedience and faith of prayer. Two such words are *shachah* and *barak*. In Genesis 22:5 Abraham tells his servants, "Stay here with the donkey; the boy and

I will go over there; we will worship, and then we will come back to you." The word translated "worship" is *shachah*, "to bow." The Hebrew word *barak* also means "to bow" and is translated by the English word "bless," "Bless the Lord, O my soul . . ." (Psalm 103:1). It is interesting to note, though, that when the word "bless" refers to a person, as in Psalm 1, "Blessed is the man . . ." (RSV), the word *asher* is used, and this means to "find the right way."

These obedience words represent the sense of awe and worship that is a vital part of the Old Testament prayer vocabulary. They signal to us that prayer is the submission of our will to the kingly reign of God. In prayer, we bow before him. We commit ourselves and our concerns to his love, and then we trust in his grace and faithfulness. This is what it means to pray in God's holy name.

The Importance of Words and Their Usage

Remember that no lexical examination of a particular word is ever complete in itself. Words are used in sentences by living people who do not carry dictionaries around as they speak. Consequently, we must always consider a word in the context of the whole sentence or paragraph. By doing this we catch the real intention of the writer's word choice. I have therefore endeavored to place each word into its biblical sentence, so that we feel it as part of a larger whole.

Nevertheless, words are essential markers, and they carry within them vital clues to the feeling level of the people who use them. We need to study words in their setting and culture, because no word ever is perfectly translated with all of its intended meanings intact. Linguistic scholars readily agree that every word has a history and an individual meaning within a language. While some overlap of meaning may exist, the idea may not be precisely conveyed in another language. This lack of precision makes biblical translation into our own language such an important and never-ending task.

By briefly examining the prayer words found in the Bible, we have explored the kinds of prayer that comprised the experience of the ancient Hebrews. We may also apply these to our own experience. When we pray, we also sing, we ask, and we try to think carefully and ponder the great truths upon which everything depends. Finally, in prayer we also must trust in the One to whom we have brought our prayers. This simply means that our words express a living relationship. They involve a communication between friends as we earnestly try to understand and seek to be understood.

3

The Language of Relationship

As a young Christian I had to unlearn the false but widely held idea that the Old Testament records God's judgment, whereas the New Testament tells the good news of God's love.

Our study of Hebrew words of prayer shows us that the God of grace is very much the God of the Old Testament. God's goodness and faithfulness stand behind all the language of approach that we tracked through the Old Testament story. Throughout Scripture, grace and judgment merge so completely that we cannot understand one without the other. The prayer language of the Bible knows the God of judgment and justice who is at the very same instant the God of kindness and forgiveness.

Dietrich Bonhoeffer put it this way: "We cannot hear the last word until we have heard the next to the last word."[1] With prayer we journey with our Judge and our Redeemer, and the fact that the God of the Bible is both

Judge and Savior makes a difference in the way we pray. The One to whom we pray understands who we really are. This total understanding is the personal significance for us of the righteous judgment of the God of the Bible. Like a great physician, this doctor really understands the full extent of the health crisis we face. For that very reason he is more useful to us than the one who has misread the symptoms, even though the less-informed doctor may have happier things to say to us.

I would rather hear the blunt and salty truth about myself, if the one who speaks can also help me find answers. Only when no answers exist would I prefer to hear only the happier words. In both the Old Testament and New Testament we hear the language of grace and realism, of God's truthful judgment and of his kindly salvation.

Now we move into the world of the New Testament writers and speakers. As they express their teaching on prayer, we observe how the deep strands of the Old Testament prayer experience emerge through New Testament Greek.

While the writers of the New Testament wrote in first-century Greek, they thought in terms of the ancient and deeply rooted Hebrew of the Old Testament. Interesting proof of this pattern is found in the Greek words chosen to express the meaning and life of prayer in the New Testament. In order to understand this it will be helpful to begin our study before the New Testament documents were written and focus on an event that occurred around 100 B.C., in Alexandria, Egypt.

Coining a New Word

At this time a group of Jewish rabbis translated the Hebrew Old Testament into Greek, because the majority of the Jews in Palestine and throughout the Mediterranean basin needed to have their Scriptures in the language commonly in use throughout the world. The Greek text these scholars produced is known as the Septuagint because, according to tradition, seventy rabbis became involved in the work.

The Septuagint had a profound effect on the New Testament Greek vocabulary. For example, the classical Greek word for "pray" at that time, *euchomai*, literally meant "to strike a bargain" with deity and described making a religious vow or a request acceptable to the gods of Greek mythology. This limited understanding served the purpose well in places like Job 22:27 (*italics mine*), "You will pray to him, and he will hear you, and you will pay your *vows*," and the translator of Malachi 1:14 also used *euchomai*, "Cursed be the cheat who has a male in the flock and *vows* to give it . . ." (*italics mine*).

But when the Septuagint rabbis wanted to more fully translate the rich meaning of the Old Testament word for "pray," they had to coin a new word, *proseuchomai*. The prefix *pros* means "to" or "toward." Adding the prefix to the classical word shifted the focus of the meaning away from the act of praying toward the One to whom we pray. In this way *euchomai* is reduced in status to the rank of a mild synonym, except where it is used in its generic sense of "vow."

New Testament Usage. The New Testament writers carefully followed the lead of the Septuagint rabbis. For example, they used the classical term in Acts 18:18, where Luke speaks of Paul cutting his hair because "he was under a vow." However, the word used overwhelmingly for "pray" in the New Testament is *proseuchomai*. "Pray toward" is the intent of Jesus' words in the Sermon on the Mount when he says, " 'When you are praying, do not heap up empty phrases as the Gentiles do; for they think they will be heard because of their many words. Do not be like them, for your Father knows what you need before you ask him. Pray then in this way: Our Father in heaven, hallowed be your name . . .' " (Matthew 6:7–9).

In addition other Greek words are joined together to describe the same five kinds of prayer found in the Old Testament vocabulary. First, there are the praise words. *Chara* means "rejoice," as in Paul's instructions to the Christians at Philippi, "Rejoice in the Lord always; again I will say, Rejoice" (Philippians 4:4). And *eucharisteo*, translated "thanksgiving," is used when Paul says to the Philippian Christians, "I thank my God every time I remember you" (Philippians 1:3). This word has a robust, songlike character to it, very much like the song words of the Old Testament Hebrew.

Two asking words for prayer appear throughout the New Testament. *Aiteo* means "to want something, to ask." This is the word Jesus gave to his disciples when he said, " 'On that day you will ask in my name . . .' " (John 16:26). An even stronger verb, *erotao*, means to ask or beg. This word was used by the Greek visitors who told Philip, " 'Sir, we wish to see Jesus' " (John 12:21). Paul used this word in the deeply moving prayer narrative about his thorn in the flesh, "Three times I appealed to the Lord about this . . ." (2 Corinthians 12:8).

The Greek prayer word *krazo* literally means "to cry" and conveys the idea of crying for help. The Apostle Paul uses this word in writing to the Roman Christians, ". . . When we cry 'Abba! Father!' it is that very Spirit bearing witness with our spirit that we are children of God" (Romans 8:15, 16). And the same "Abba! Father!" cry re-echoes in Paul's letter to the Christians in Galatia (Galatians 4:6).

The Greek prayer word *proskuneo* also strongly echoes the Old Testament. It means "to bow" and is used in a decisive way in the fourth Gospel, where it is translated by the English word "worship": "But the hour is coming, and is now here, when the true worshipers will worship the Father in spirit and truth, for the Father seeks such as these to worship him" (John 4:23).

We'll mention two more words that are used for prayer. *Epikaleo* means "to call and express confession." This appears in the story of Ananias of Damascus, when the Lord told him about Saul of Tarsus, who was on Straight Street, waiting for deliverance from the blindness that had struck him when the Lord spoke to him on the Damascus road. In response to the Lord's instructions, Ananias said, "Lord, I have heard from many about this man, how much evil he has done to your saints in Jerusalem; and here he has authority . . . to bind all who invoke ["who call upon," *epikaleo*] your name" (Acts 9:13, 14). Finally, we have *deomai*, which is used to express specific prayer requests. Paul uses this word in writing to the Christians at Philippi, "Do not worry about anything, but in everything by prayer and supplication with thanksgiving let your requests be made known to God" (Philippians 4:6).

As we observed in our examination of the Old Testament prayer words, vocabulary has no life of its own, apart from its use in sentences and paragraphs. If we are to understand what prayer means in the Bible, we must watch the words as they connect with life. When we see people pray and when we listen closely to our Lord as he teaches his followers about prayer, we will learn the meaning of prayer and understand it as the language of our friendship with him.

Praying Toward the Lord

There remains one more part of the puzzle. To really understand prayer, we must begin ourselves to pray *toward the Lord.* When we are doing that, we will perceive with greater clarity what we mean when we praise, when we call for help, when we ask, when we think through human concerns with God, and when we bow in worship—accepting God's will as we pray in Jesus' name. In this way, we will learn ourselves firsthand about praying toward the Lord as we actually do it.

Part II

The Nature of the Friendship

4

The Prayer–Songs of Our Lives

If you want to get to know me as a person better, one of the very best ways is to hear the songs that have influenced my life. In my childhood my father sang to our family, songs that made me feel secure. I especially remember "Bye Baby Bunting" and "Old Spinning Wheel." Hymns such as "Jesus Loves Me" and the Christmas carols made a strong impression on my life from the earliest days, before I was consciously a Christian believer.

During my high-school years my favorite song was the slow waltz "Dream," because that was always the last one played at our school dances. In college the brash and boldly rhythmic big bands were my favorite. At this time I also began a lifelong love affair with Broadway musicals—I enjoyed music that told a story. Classical music became important to me while I was a student in college. And Handel's *Messiah* completely won me body and soul before I understood its profound biblical message. Today my favorites include music by composers like Tchaikovsky, Grieg, Rachmaninoff, Gershwin, Beethoven, Mozart, and Bach.

Now that my children are young adults, I can see that my favorite music has become their music. Many of the songs they call their own are the ones they learned from their mother and me. Their music has become mine as well. You can tell my story and the story of our family by the songs and hymns that have traveled with us in good times and hard times and all the average day-to-day times in between.

Songs Tell a Story

Even as songs reveal part of the story of who people are, they also tell the story of nations and civilizations. This is certainly true in coming to a better understanding of the history of the United States. First came the early songs sung by native Americans around village campfires. Then followed the songs introduced by early European colonists, songs that emerged through the American Revolutionary War. These are followed by songs that told the story of a growing and expanding nation.

Our history is enriched by the spirituals sung by the African-American slaves and by the antislavery songs that spoke of deliverance. Songs and hymns emerged through the great religious awakening—the revivals—of the late 1800s. Patriotic songs of the First and Second World Wars followed. The American scene comes to life through jazz, the blues, cowboy melodies, country music, and beloved gospel songs. Yes, we can learn a great deal about ourselves and our heritage by listening to the music that has held our attention and given us feelings of joy and well-being.

The Bible and Its Prayer–Songs

In a similar way, the people of our Bible—the Old and New Testaments—were passionately influenced by the prayer–songs, that were so much a part of their history. The Book of Psalms, the prayer–song book of the Old Testament, tells about God and his actions in human history. In this magnificent collection we are able to participate in their hopes, their fears, their successes and defeats.

Not only in the Book of Psalms do we find songs and prayer–songs in Scripture. From the Book of Job to the Book of Revelation—throughout our entire Bible, in fact—we find grand songs and chorales and prayer–songs of praise, hope, worry, complaint, and trust. In the objective prayer–songs God has revealed himself and his character.

A second group of prayer–songs are subjective. These tell stories—sometimes joyous, other times stormy—of our own journey of faith, of our personal reactions to that journey, and of our personal experiences with God's character, as well as our experience with the world in which we live. For example, Psalm 107 tells four short stories about people who wandered around in the desert, who were in prison, who were sick, and who were caught in devastating storms. In each instance the Psalmist writes that they "cried to the Lord in their trouble, and he delivered them from their distress" (Psalm 107:6, 13, 19, 28).

A third group of prayer–songs are those of intercession: "To you, O Lord, I lift up my soul," writes David in Psalm 25. "O my God, in you I trust; do not let me be put to shame; do not let my enemies exult over me." These prayer–songs of request combine both objective and subjective feelings. Here David expressed his personal condition, ". . . I am lonely and afflicted. Relieve the troubles of my heart . . ." (Psalm 25:16, 17). At the same time he expressed his objective convictions about the character of God: "Good and upright is the Lord; therefore he instructs sinners in the way" (Psalm 25:8).

A fourth group of prayer–songs might be labeled the songs of joy—the shouting songs. Here, too, we have a response to the character of God. An example is found in the opening words of Psalm 147, "Praise the Lord! How good it is to sing praises to our God; for he is gracious, and a song of praise is fitting."

In vivid contrast to these are the grieving prayer–songs, or those of lamentation—the uncomfortable and angry-sounding prayer–songs of the Old Testament. A striking example of these is found in Psalm 137, "By the rivers of Babylon—there we sat down and there we wept when we remembered Zion. . . . For there our captors asked us for songs . . . , 'Sing us one of the songs of Zion!' How could we sing the Lord's song in a foreign land?"

There are also the hosanna prayer–songs, literally the "help, please," the "cry for help" songs. David writes, "Save me, O God, by your name, and vindicate me by your might. Hear my prayer, O God. . . . For the insolent have risen against me, the ruthless seek my life; they do not set God before them" (Psalm 54:1–3).

Finally, there are the prayer–songs of meditation, the *haga* prayers, the songs of humming. Here, we hum over in our heads and hearts the great themes of God's character. A magnificent *haga* prayer–song finds expression in Psalm 23, "The Lord is my shepherd, I shall not want. . . ."

It is important to note that within the New Testament writings the most-quoted Old Testament selections are the prayer poetry of the Book of Psalms. These quotations become fundamental building blocks in New Testament teaching. The messianic claims of Jesus are founded upon the words of the psalmic prayer–songs as much as upon the writings of law and prophecy.

For example, in Matthew 21 we have the narrative of our Lord in a tense moment when his messiahship was severely contested. Contained in this moving scene is one of the most important theological speeches Jesus ever gave—a discourse carefully built upon quotations from the Psalms. Here Jesus said, " 'Have you never read in the scriptures: "The stone that the builders rejected has become the cornerstone; this was the Lord's doing, and it is amazing in our eyes"?' " (Matthew 21:42).

Here Jesus utilized words from Psalm 118:22, 23, that section of the Psalms the Jews called the *Hallel* (Psalms 113–118). They were the most important group of public prayers used for Jewish worship in the Old Testament, and they were sung during such high feasts as Passover and the Feast of Tabernacles. Jesus quoted decisively from these prayers and built his messianic claim upon the promises and predictions found within the *Hallel*, as he identified himself as "the chief cornerstone," the one the builders rejected.

The most famous of all psalmic prayer quotations in the New Testament was uttered by our Lord during his darkest hour on the cross: " 'My God, my God, why have you forsaken me? . . .' " This is one of the few places in the New Testament where the Gospel writers record Jesus speaking in Aramaic, the northern dialect of his youth. The people of Judah, who were standing around the cross did not understand Jesus' Aramaic quotation from the opening words of Psalm 22 and thought he instead was asking for Elijah. But this was not the case, as in his agony Jesus called out to his heavenly Father in the language of his boyhood.

Psalm 103

A Prayer–Song of Worship. It is important to our understanding of these psalmic prayer–songs for us to remember that all the subjective ones have their foundation secured in the objective ones. Remember, an objective psalm states great facts about who God is; the objective affirmation also has a profoundly subjective element, simply because objective truth always creates a strong subjective response when we really believe what we sing and pray. But before we either praise God or cry out to him for help, we depend upon the foundational truth that God stands beneath every prayer–song. In coming to a clearer understanding of this truth, let's take a close look at a classic example of an objective psalm:

Bless the Lord, O my soul,
  and all that is within me, bless his holy name.
Bless the Lord, O my soul,
  and do not forget all his benefits—
who forgives all your iniquity,
  who heals all your diseases,
who redeems your life from the Pit,

who crowns you with steadfast love and mercy,
who satisfies you with good as long as you live
so that your youth is renewed like the eagle's.
Psalm 103:1–5

Now, this psalm begins with the word *bless*, translated from the Hebrew word *barak*, which means "to bow." In other words, this actually reads, "I bow to the Lord and to his holy name." As we have seen, "bless" is a word for worship, and this psalm begins and ends with that thought.

Next, we ask, "Why does David bow before the Lord?" He does, we read, because God forgives all our iniquities, because he heals all of our diseases, and because he redeems our lives from the Pit. Notice now that David is recounting the objective and durable facts about God. God crowns us with steadfast love and mercy. And he is the One who satisfies us with good as long as we live so that our youth is renewed like the eagle's.

About three hundred years after David wrote this psalm, the Book of Isaiah was written. Yet if we read Psalm 103:15, we see its influence upon Isaiah, 40:6, ". . . All people are grass. . . ." Then notice the similarity between the final paragraph of this chapter of Isaiah and Psalm 103:5. The prophet writes: "Even youths will faint and be weary, and the young will fall exhausted; but those who wait for the Lord shall renew their strength, they shall mount up with wings like eagles . . ." (Isaiah 40:30, 31). From this literary comparison, we can begin to see how many Old Testament prophets built songs and prayers upon the Book of Psalms' foundation.

God's Acts on Behalf of the Oppressed. In the second movement of Psalm 103, verses 6–14, we are told that the Lord acts in vindication and judgment for all oppressed people. Note the wording of this magnificent prayer–song:

The Lord works vindication
  and justice for all who are oppressed.
He made known his ways to Moses,
  his acts to the people of Israel.
The Lord is merciful and gracious,
  slow to anger and abounding in steadfast love.
He will not always accuse,
  nor will he keep his anger forever.
He does not deal with us according to our sins,
  nor repay us according to our iniquities.
For as the heavens are high above the earth,
  so great is his steadfast love
    toward those who fear him;
as far as the east is from the west,
  so far he removes our transgressions from us.
As a father has compassion for his children,
  so the Lord has compassion for those who fear him.
For he knows how we were made;
  he remembers that we are dust.

Psalm 103:6–14

Here we are told the objective fact that the Lord is merciful and gracious, and we discover this truth about God by what he says and by what he does. Such a fundamental truth will give us confidence when we pray. I have to believe that the Apostle Paul was influenced by this theme when he wrote these vivid words of hope to the Christians at Rome:

> Who will separate us from the love of Christ? Will hardship, or distress, or persecution, or famine, or nakedness, or peril, or sword? As it is written,
>
> "For your sake we are being
> killed all day long;
> we are accounted as sheep to
> be slaughtered."
>
> No, in all these things we are more than conquerors through him who loved us. For I am convinced that neither death, nor life, nor angels, nor rulers, nor things present, nor things to come, nor powers, nor height, nor depth, nor anything else in all creation, will be able to separate us from the love of God in Christ Jesus our Lord.
>
> Romans 8:35–39

Our Weakness Versus God's Generosity. The next movement of Psalm 103 contrasts the frailty of people with the God who loves his children and gives them good gifts:

> As for mortals, their days are like grass;
> they flourish like a flower of the field;
> for the wind passes over it, and it is gone,
> and its place knows it no more.
> But the steadfast love of the Lord is from everlasting
> to everlasting on those who fear him,
> and his righteousness to children's children,
> to those who keep his covenant and remember
> to do his commandments.
>
> Psalm 103:15–18

At the same time this is a psalm about the law. It is about God's will and our responsibility to obey the revelation of his will. Further, it speaks about God's faithfulness and love. We also catch the contrast between God's strength and our frailty as the psalm writer compares the human family to grass that is here today and gone tomorrow. Our lives lack permanence in themselves, but the character and promises of God stand forever.

God's Stability in a Changing World. In the final movement of this powerful prayer–song the psalmist writes:

> The Lord has established his throne in the heavens,
> and his kingdom rules over all.
> Bless the Lord, O you his angels,
> you mighty ones who do his bidding,
> obedient to his spoken word.
> Bless the Lord, all his hosts,
> his ministers that do his will.
> Bless the Lord, all his works,
> in all places of his dominion.
> Bless the Lord, O my soul.
>
> Psalm 103:19–22

In these concluding sentences we have a prayer–song of very deep feeling that is objective in form and content as the writer describes the fundamental issue of God's stability in a world of change.

Wanted! A Personal Response. As we reflect on this psalmic prayer–song, we will do well to ask, "How should we respond to this psalm? What does this prayer–song say to us about our own prayers?" To bring my own reflections into sharper focus, I must ask, "Is this the prayer–song of my life? Would I have written something like this?" Indeed, these penetrating questions call for prayerful response!

Our family has always enjoyed playing the game *Trivial Pursuit*. Recently I was stumped by a question about when the Olympic Games were held in Mexico City. This lapse disturbed me, because I have always been an avid follower of the various Olympic contests. Then I realized that while Olympic dates of themselves are interesting, they are not permanently memorable. In fact, every human date and event is in the final analysis like the blade of grass spoken of in the psalm—like grass they finally fade away. Sooner or later the games we play and the game scores fade from our memories. Because of this universal "memory fade-out" we need objective psalmic prayer–songs in our lives that remind us of a reality not like yesterday's statistics—faded if not totally forgotten.

This leads me to narrow my question even further, "Do I have objective prayer–songs for my life? Or do I rely primarily on 'feeling' prayer–songs?" If my response indicates that my prayer–songs center mostly on my feelings, I am forced to confront this objective question, "What is true today or tomorrow, regardless of how I feel?" The answer comes through to me loud and clear that Psalm 103 lays before me the eternal truth so essential to my existence: We may be like the grass the psalmist speaks of; but two things remain durable—God's justice/truth and his love/forgiveness are facts that will stand for all time. These give eternal meaning to friendship with God.

I am convinced that we all need both durable prayer–songs and the up-and-down subjective ones. We live everyday with ups and downs. In the midst of these, we need objective reality that stands when everything else is dried out by the winds that plague our human existence. Unless prayer has godward objectiveness, it is only an inner attitude exercise of religious sentiment and feeling.

That is what *pros*, the "toward" prefix, in *proseuchomai*, "pray toward," is all about. The Septuagint translators, over two thousand years ago, understood the importance of using prayer words that would shift our attention away from a preoccupation with techniques of prayer toward "to whom" we pray. Without the God who is *really* there, our prayers would only be interior mood changes with a religious flavor. Imagine! He who made the marvel of the human ear is himself able to hear our prayers! This means that prayer is profoundly personal, for God is personal, and at the very core of this communication reality is his living personhood and character.

At the same time the prayer–songs of the Bible are wonderfully subjective as well. The prayers of the Book of Psalms and those throughout all of the Bible resonate with our own lives. At times they do so with more accuracy than any other part of Scripture.

A friend told me that during a very difficult period in his life the only part of Scripture he could read was the Bible's prayer–song book—the Psalms. Their rhythm of realism and hope and their honest admission of grief mixed with praise nourished him. This book of prayer met him at the point of his deepest need, of his deepest feelings. His choice to live in the Psalms was right, for there he saw who God is. The surprise for him was that he met the objective Lord of grace and truth at the core of these highly personal and honest prayer–songs of the soul.

When we pray, God invites us to enter into the vast

cathedral of great objective truths about himself. We discover the deeply personal language of our friendship with God and participate in the reality that "the steadfast love of the Lord is from everlasting to everlasting. . ." (Psalm 103:17)

5

Prayer and Meditation: Keys to Survival

In these closing days of the twentieth century we live in the convenience of a communication revolution, and one symbol of this massive change is the VCR—a machine that is drastically altering the life-style of millions of families. With this marvelous contraption you can attend an evening church meeting or the PTA and not miss your favorite television program. At one time a missed program was gone forever, but not now.

Between television and the VCR we are caught in a massive communications overload that can so easily absorb every waking moment. In times of crisis, with the aid of satellites and movie films, we instantly become involved in news in the Middle East or Asia or Africa. With the amazing array of modern communication technology, we also become participants in events occurring in the outreaches of space.

Never before have people been subjected to both the

marvel and the curse of our current communication and media capabilities. So how do we cope? How do we live in a world where there is so much media stimulus? How do we make sense out of our twenty-four-hour days and maintain our perspective in the midst of the colossal flood of impressions that stagger our minds and emotions? How do we steer a course through all of this and still arrive at the most important goals of our lives? How do we arrive at the end of each day with a handle on who we are as Christians, as husbands or wives or parents or friends?

The Focus Principle

Confronting the art of creative living in an electronic age is not unlike the challenge that faces an Olympic athlete in gymnastic events. For both balance is so crucial. Watching a gymnast performing on parallel bars in a huge stadium, packed with a noisy and enthusiastic crowd, I always feel awe. Uppermost in my mind is the question, *How does a gymnast execute those precise routines in the middle of such confusion*?

Closer to home, I have often wondered how, just moments before closing time, my mechanic can diagnose the mysterious ailment plaguing my car. Then there's the surgeon who performs a delicate operation, sometimes even under a microscope, in the glare of blinding lights and in front of restless medical students. We've all observed the secretary working doggedly to complete a priority project while being constantly interrupted by telephone calls.

How do these "ordinary" people accomplish their tasks under such high-pressure circumstances? The answer is not all that complicated: They do what they have to do, irrespective of their surroundings, by focusing their attention and concentration upon a few important tasks. These people have learned how to "major on the majors and minor on the minors" by putting any distracting elements out of their minds.

In talking with some of my scuba-diving friends, I learned that a diver can so easily become disoriented fifty feet below the surface. Believe me, this would be no time to panic, so every diver is trained to remember three things: Look for your partner, search the water for his or her air bubbles, and then ascend slowly. Everything else, especially sickening waves of panic, must be put out of the diver's mind in favor of the most important facts.

The truth is that most of us can handle any pressure when we learn to focus, and this principle can transform our prayer life. Our study of the prayers and prayer–songs of the Bible is so important to our own prayer journey, because these prayers and prayer–songs focus on God's character, on objective truth.

At the same time, though, these prayers contain a subjective element, describing our feelings and experiences—those common to our daily struggle for meaning. When we read a prayer–song about grief or fear or joy, we identify with the psalmist's words and feelings. When we subjectively examine our complaints, our grief, our joy, our hurt of any kind—all of which may be valid—they must fit into a larger framework—the objective foundation of God's nature. Otherwise they may cause us to be distracted at a time of vulnerability.

I've realized that it is impossible for me to keep perspective when I become the center of my own attention. Instead I need a plan for focusing, for maintaining a proper perspective. Each of us must catch the truth that meditation in the Bible is in reality the simple act of focusing. The psalmist expressed it, "Let the words of my mouth and the *meditation* of my heart be acceptable to you, O Lord, my rock and my redeemer" (Psalm 19:14, *italics mine*).

As we seek to understand what meditation means in our individual prayer journeys, we must abolish the idea that it means emptying our minds. Some seminars and self-realization courses have tried to sell us on the myth that when we are under stress we should shift our minds into neutral: We are to relax and coast and clear our minds completely.

When I have become particularly fatigued or overloaded with pressure, a natural inclination has encouraged me to clear or empty my mind of thoughts and worries. But Scripture describes a better way.

At such times I have learned I need a mind that is able to focus on the great truths about God's character and his promises, and the Bible's prayer–song book offers the help I need to accomplish this. The biblical teaching about meditation points toward the great truths: We are to clarify our minds rather than empty them. Just as the disoriented scuba diver doesn't need an empty mind, but one focused on finding his or her partner and then following the air bubbles to the surface, we need the guidance of God's Word.

Will a parent facing a crisis with a child who needs assurance of love engage in a mind-emptying exercise? Not if he or she has the child's best interests at heart. Instead, the parent needs a clear mind—one that immediately is present and quick to give assurance of love and caring. To hesitate or withdraw at such times may well result in a missed opportunity.

A Focused Mind and Meditative Prayer

A focused mind—one saturated with meditative prayer—helps us distinguish the important in life from the less important. Happily, the Bible offers us a rich tradition of prayer as meditative focusing, and Scripture includes a great deal of teaching that helps us understand and practice the prayer of meditation.

Psalm 77 is a marvelous prayer–song in the meditation tradition of the Bible. It gives us a rich and diverse vocabulary of focusing and shows us that focusing has nothing to do with the myth of emptying our minds. Rather, this psalm emphasizes clarifying our minds, attuning them so we can concentrate on the two or three most vital truths of the moment. Then we can place our feelings in the context of those great truths.

The Feelings of a Prayer–Song Writer. In reading this psalm, we confront all of the emotions of the subjective psalms; we hear the psalmist's complaint and his cry of near panic; at the beginning, we confront his disorientation as the writer tries to express his feelings in a time of harrowing stress.

Sheer terror fills the opening words of the psalm. But gradually, after giving vent to anger, dismay, and self-doubt, the writer remembers God and his mighty deeds. In that remembering, he discovers a solid hope. But first, the panic:

> I cry aloud to God,
> aloud to God, that he may hear me.
> In the day of my trouble I seek the Lord;
> in the night my hand is stretched
> out without wearying;
> my soul refuses to be comforted.
>
> Psalm 77:1, 2

We catch an overpowering sense of catastrophe here, and the writer seems to feel he must scream, if God is to hear him. Notice, he can't relax at night as he stretches out his hand in an effort to find and touch God. In varying degrees most of us have felt that way. We've experienced those hours of darkness, when our souls could find no comfort and nothing and no one was there to help. This is a powerful description of depression.

Now the psalmist continues:

> I think of God, and I moan;
> I meditate, and my spirit faints.
> You keep my eyelids from closing;
> I am so troubled that I cannot speak.
> I consider the days of old,
> and remember the years of long ago.
> I commune with my heart in the night;
> I meditate and search my spirit:
> "Will the lord spurn forever,
> and never again be favorable?
> Has his steadfast love ceased forever?
> Are his promises at an end for all time?
> Has God forgotten to be gracious?
> Has he in anger shut up his compassion?"
> And I say, "It is my grief
> that the right hand of the Most High has changed."
>
> Psalm 77:3–10

In these words the prayer–song writer looks inward and outward at the same moment as he gets in touch with the complexity of his feelings. It is fascinating to note that he uses almost all the love vocabulary of the Old Testament in these verses. But he wonders if that grace is there for him and asks if God has any compassion toward him. We can't help but feel something of the writer's anger and fear of his own powerlessness.

Airplane pilots sometimes fly into what they term a "white out"; they lose all orientation. They may feel they are flying upside-down, when in reality they are right-side up. At such times they can't rely on their senses but must depend entirely on their instruments.

Have you ever entered, as I have, a long "white out" of the soul? If so, spiritually you were not quite sure whether you were upside-down or right-side up. When Christians feel bombarded on every side, how do we keep perspective? What do we do?

The answer comes through clearly: We focus as the psalmist does. Up to this point he has expressed his feelings. Had he ended the prayer–song now, it would offer no help or hope—not for him and certainly not for us. But there's more.

Three Important Prayer Words

As we move into the second half of the psalm, notice three great words of focusing: *remember, meditate,* and *muse.*

I will call to mind the deeds of the Lord;
  I will *remember* your wonders of old.
I will *meditate* on all your work,
  and *muse* on your mighty deeds.
Your way, O God, is holy.
  What god is so great as our God?
You are the God who works wonders;
  you have displayed your might among the peoples.

With your strong arm you redeemed your people,
the descendents of Jacob and Joseph. *Selah*

Psalm 77:11–15, *italics mine*

In order to capture the prayer–song's full implication, we need to probe further into the three words: *remember, meditate* and *muse*. The Hebrew word translated "I will remember" in verse 11 is *zakar*—the same word was translated "meditate" in verses 3 and 6. The word translated "meditate" in verse 12 is the Hebrew *siah*, a word used by actors that means "to rehearse" or "to think through the implications." We might distinguish these two words by saying that *zakar* means to remember the lines, and *siah* means to rehearse. Both are essential for effective prayer–meditation.

These words were illuminated for me a few years ago when I had a part in a play. Before any of us actors could work on the interpretation of our lines, we had to learn them. Our director drove this point home: "I want you to know your lines so well that when one character finishes his speech, the next actor, without even a second thought or hesitation, moves right into the next line. We will not be ready to interpret until each actor knows the lines flawlessly. Only when you really know your lines can you work on the nuances. Then we will not only know what the words say but what they mean. Only then can we add the subtle intonations and meanings."

The third word, "muse," is the Hebrew *haga*, referred to earlier, which literally means "to hum." We not only remember and rehearse the lines of our prayer–song, we hum them in the deepest recesses of our souls. They are a part of us physically, emotionally, and spiritually.

An apt modern analogy to this appears in the actions of a well-oiled football team in which every player must know the various plays so well that he moves instinctively into the right position and formation as soon as the play is called. Everything he has learned and rehearsed becomes automatic as each player makes his move, in spite of the efforts of the other team to frustrate the game plan.

In this way, a football game becomes a surprising and highly charged parable of prayer–meditation—we so remember the truth of God's forgiveness and goodness, we so rehearse the reality of his grace and goodness that it becomes a part of us. We know it; we live it—from the inside out. Prayer–meditation springs up from the deepest recesses of our beings and becomes the prayer language of our friendship with God.

Finally, the Hebrew word *selah*, found at the end of verse 15, adds to this imagery. While this word appears several times throughout the Book of Psalms, language and biblical scholars have never agreed on its meaning. It has been suggested that it likely was some form of instruction for musicians or worshipers in the Jerusalem Temple. We do, however, have one textual clue as to what it may mean at the end of verse 16 of Psalm 9, where the Hebrew reads, *higion selah*. We know that the root of *higion* is *haga*, which means "to hum." If this is the case, we have the instruction to hum—meditate—on the meaning of the prayer–song, that has literally become a part of us. Danish theologian and philosopher Søren Kierkegaard expressed the same idea when he wrote, "I don't know the truth until it becomes a part of me."

The association of *selah* with "hum" and "meditation"

makes a lot of sense. We hum the tunes that arise from our deepest selves. As we remember, meditate, and muse in our prayer pilgrimage, like the writer of this prayer–song, we will focus on those enduring realities of life with God. Though the psalm writer openly expressed his pain and overwhelming grief, at a certain moment he deliberately and consciously says, "I will call to mind. . . ." His mind is flooded with God's actions in the past, and he determines at that moment to concentrate and meditate on them.

For all of us the good news is that the God who redeemed this prayer–song writer is our redeemer, too. That is something to remember, to rehearse, and to hum about—something to prayerfully reflect on and meditate about, as we shut out the distractions of our technologically noisy world.

At this point I remember what happened long ago in the Jerusalem upper room, when Jesus celebrated the Last Supper with his disciples. For as we participate in this sacred rite, as Jesus commanded—"Do this until I come"—we celebrate these three great facts that we are encouraged to remember, to rehearse, and to hum.

1. We are to remember that our Lord has, once and for all, won the victory over death, sin, and the devil.
2. We remember it was a costly victory—our Lord suffered and died for us. That is why we experience feelings of deep pathos and even grief as we eat the bread and drink the wine in remembrance of his broken body and shed blood.
3. We remember that the resurrected Jesus is our Redeemer—he is alive and with us now. As we remember and focus—prayerfully meditate—on

this compelling truth, we sense his real presence with us. Indeed the Eucharist is a New Testament means of focusing.

The Apostle Paul and a Strategy for Focusing

Writing to his Christian friends at Philippi, the Apostle Paul lays out a strategy for focusing that follows closely what we have discovered in the psalmic prayer–songs. He keenly understands the need for the Philippian Christians and us to cry out to God in prayer and to express our feelings, whatever they may be. But he follows all of this with an exhortation to meditate on God's goodness and faithfulness:

> Rejoice in the Lord always; again I will say, Rejoice. Let your gentleness be known to everyone. The Lord is near. Do not worry about anything, but in everything by prayer and supplication let your requests be made known to God. And the peace of God, which surpasses all understanding, will guard your hearts and your minds in Christ Jesus.
>
> Finally, beloved, whatever is true, whatever is honorable, whatever is just, whatever is pure, whatever is pleasing, whatever is commendable, if there is any excellence and if there is anything worthy of praise, *think about these things.*
>
> Philippians 4:4–8, *italics mine*

Indeed, as, through prayerful meditation, we focus on the goodness of the Lord and the truth " 'his steadfast love endures forever' " (Psalm 118), we link up with the people of God in all of time, described by the prayer–song writer with these words:

Happy are those whose help is the God of Jacob,
whose hope is in the Lord their God,
who made heaven and earth,
the sea, and all that is in them;
who keeps faith forever. . . .
Praise the Lord!

Psalm 146:5, 6, 10

6

Who Is There When We Pray?

The people of the Bible—our spiritual ancestors—constantly struggled to maintain a relationship with a God they could not see. Throughout the centuries of human existence, people have wrestled with the reality of God. Our human pragmatic mind-set cries out for concrete proof that God is—that there is really someone out there who hears us when we pray.

Questions That Won't Go Away

In our better moments we echo the feelings and sentiments of the Bible's prayer–song writers, but in the nitty-gritty give-and-take of life another side of us cries out for proof that the God to whom we pray actually exists. Prayer forces these questions of our minds and feelings to center stage, and for this reason the existence of God and the proofs of his existence are old questions that just won't go away.

Again, in our better moments and at the very starting place in our praying, we trust that God is real and powerful; yet when we attempt to give convincing proofs to anyone who questions us, the explanations and proofs seem weak to them. In his *Screwtape Letters,* C. S. Lewis, a brilliant British writer and theologian, has his senior devil, Screwtape, wrestling with the question of why God does not make dramatic use of his almighty power and thereby prove once and for all that he is there. Finally, Screwtape comments to Wormwood, a junior devil, "You must have often wondered why the Enemy [God] does not make more use of his power . . . but you now see that the Irresistible and the Indisputable are the two weapons which the very nature of his scheme forbids him to use . . . He cannot 'tempt' to virtue as we do to vice."[1]

Most certainly we do not have a pragmatic proof for God that sweeps away every question. In Greek mythology, Zeus, the head god, always overwhelmed people and the lesser gods by his power. But we do not experience such proofs from God the Father of the Lord Jesus Christ. Instead we have just enough evidence to assure us of the love, the integrity, and the faithfulness of Jesus Christ. On the basis of that evidence, we believe and pray.

Can I Have Absolute Proof?

During the years when I was minister to students at University Presbyterian Church, in Seattle, a young man came to me for help and counsel. He was struggling with very serious doubts about God. After we talked at considerable length, I asked him what would help him the most at this stage of his struggle.

"I'd need absolute proof of God's existence," he replied.

I then asked my young friend what kind of proof would satisfy him, and I promised to attempt to respond. He leaned back in his chair, looked out the window of my office, pointed to a tree on the church grounds, and said, "If I could see that tree split in two by lightning at exactly 12:05 this afternoon, I would consider that proof positive of God's existence."

After thinking about his request for a few moments, I looked him straight in the eyes. "Okay, let us suppose that it is now 12:06 this afternoon, and the tree is split cleanly by lightning," I responded. "Everything has happened just as you described it. What has your 'proof' proved?"

A prolonged silence greeted my question.

Then I added, "I think the split tree would only prove the existence of some mysterious spiritual power that for whatever reason chose to amuse a couple of human beings on Northeast Forty-fifth Street and possibly even deceive them."

While I didn't mention it at the time, the split tree could also have been the result of an incredible coincidence. But the truth is that there is no proof of the kind this student thought he wanted—absolute proof of the existence of God. Certainly a tree split by lightning on the campus of University Presbyterian Church at 12:05 in the afternoon would not possibly tell us anything about the character of God—about either his love or his faithfulness.

My exchange with that university student illuminates the dilemma we face when we make a demand for absolute reasons and assurances from God. Any "absolute" proof falls short because in the words of Blaise Pascal, seventeenth-century Christian and French philosopher, "We do not trust our senses." Each new day would call for more dramatic proof to prop up a misplaced faith. Absolutes are impossible for us to design or experience. Our imagination is never satisfied precisely because *we are not absolute* and never will be.

Only God is absolute, and that is why there are no absolute proofs of his existence that we humans can fathom. The so-called absolute proof that my friend thought he wanted turned out to be neither absolute nor proof. This sort of thing doesn't really prove any of the important things that God wants us to know. In no way could such an act express the deepest realities of who God is or what he does.

No, Almighty God cannot be "proved," because he is too vast to prove. But here is the great good news—God is not too vast to make himself known to us! And this he does.

Happily, as we have moved steadily toward the end of the twentieth century, with its amazing record of technological achievements that have opened up staggering secrets of both our world and the universe, we have reached the place where the existence of God is not the central question. The evidence of science and nature is too overwhelming. Both quantum mechanics and Einsteinian physics have brought us into a recognition that the universe has experienced what Stephen Hawking in *A Brief History of Time* has called "the extraordinarily vast" and the "extraordinarily tiny." This amazing mixture of discoveries has made the comment of astronomer Sir James Jeans more relevant than ever: "There is a cheater in the universe."

Clearly probability and the laws of randomness cannot explain existence to us in any way that will satisfy the mind of either the philosopher or the physicist. Consequently, science compels us to ponder creation by decision—the deliberate act of a divine Creator. In my search for understanding and in my prayer pilgrimage, I can accept the fact of the existence of a Creator because I see so much evidence of his handiwork in creation. Yet somehow I need something else; I need to understand the will behind the Creator's actions and decisions.

Who Is There?

When I was twelve years old, my family lived in McCloud, California, a small lumber town perched on the lower reaches of Mount Shasta, in the northern part of the state. In due course I joined Troop 42 of the Boy Scouts of America. As a Tenderfoot Scout my initiation was to complete a two-and-one-half-mile hike in the dead of night from the troop's campsite back to the town of McCloud. But here was the catch—I had to go it alone and without the use of a light of any kind. Believe me, the nights are really black in that isolated and remote part of the country.

I still have vivid recollections of that scary journey and several experiences of stark terror, when I heard a movement or any strange sound. My imagination ran wild, and more than once I froze at what sounded like footsteps while I strained in vain to pierce the dense darkness.

That night I made the important discovery that the question of the "existence" of something in the underbrush near me was nowhere near important as "who" might be lurking nearby. My boyish mind had no difficulty in feeling that a certain something or someone was there, because I could hear the evidence of sound. But of signal importance to me was the "who" behind those sounds. Was it a bear? a timid deer? a prowling skunk? or a person? To carry the illustration to its central point, I got absolutely no assurance from any proofs about the reality of something making noises. I wanted more; it was the "who" that really mattered. In the same way for me and my generation it isn't enough to know that God or some first source of creation power exists. Rather the significant information in my intellectual journey of faith is the character of the God who exists.

Once this distinction became clear, I was convinced that the writers of the Bible are quite correct in their apparent lack of concern about offering proof of the prior existence of God. Instead, the prayer–songs and narratives in Scripture totally focus on revealing the character of the God who exists. This across-the-board concern surfaces throughout the entire Bible, as every prayer text in Scripture addresses this vital question: Who is there when I dare to pray?

A God of Law *and* Grace

The objective psalms are not intended as proof or absolute statements that define who God is or what he must do. Rather, these prayer–songs point toward God's self-disclosure of his character, as illuminated in his covenants and law—those promises God gives us as revealed in the law and gospel of Jesus Christ.

Psalm 119, a superb example of an objective psalm, is known as a Torah song—a song of law. It points to God's self-disclosure of his will in the law and focuses on the character of the God of the law, who is also the God of grace.

God has already made the promises of that self-disclosure clear in both the convenant and law and through the One who fulfilled all his laws and covenants—his Son, Jesus Christ.

With this truth firmly fixed in our minds, we pray not only to the God of mystery and holy freedom but to the God who has shown us his profound personhood. Notice in these few lines from Psalm 119 how this, the longest of the Torah songs, points toward the Lord of our prayers:

"Teach me, O Lord, the way of your statutes,
  and I will observe it to the end.
Give me understanding, that I may keep your law
  and observe it with my whole heart.
Lead me in the path of your commandments,
  for I delight in it.
Turn my heart to your decrees,
  and not to selfish gain.
Turn my eyes from looking at vanities;
  give me life in your ways.
Confirm to your servant your promise,
  which is for those who fear you.
Turn away the disgrace that I dread,
  for your ordinances are good.
See, I have longed for your precepts;
  in your righteousness give me life.
Let your steadfast love come to me, O Lord,
  your salvation according to your promise.

Psalm 119:33–41

The prayer–song writer emphasizes the law of God as the good promise given us of God's love toward us. Consequently, as we pray this prayer, we express our desire to walk in the way of God's will.

As we follow the psalmist's response to the divine disclosure, we receive a framework of knowledge of God's nature and learn his will for us. Then we can intercede and make requests of the Lord who not only knows us, but whom we know, too.

Further along, the psalm writer prays for help—and so do we—in understanding God and his ways:

> Your hands have made and fashioned me;
> give me understanding that I may learn
> your commandments.
>
> Psalm 119:73

Note the final, urgent words of the psalm as with powerful realism the songwriter pleads for help:

> Let your hand be ready to help me,
> for I have chosen your precepts.
> I long for your salvation, O Lord,
> and your law is my delight.
> Let me live that I may praise you,
> and let your ordinances help me.
> I have gone astray like a lost sheep;
> seek out your servant,
> for I do not forget your commandments.
>
> Psalm 119:173–176

The writer asked for help on the basis of the objective self-disclosure of God's love and justice, as shown in the convenant made on Mount Sinai with the people of Israel, and he expressed deep yearning for the good news of God's covenant of grace alongside his covenant of law. This very mixture of grace and truth inevitably results in our prayer, when we center only on God himself.

As I personalize the marvelous truth that comes through in this psalmic prayer–song, I readily acknowledge my need for such prayer. Not only do I require the prayer that suspects God's existence, I need the kind of prayer that wagers on the God of love who cares deeply, as a loving Friend, about a twelve-year-old boy picking his way along in the dark, fearful of the unknown night sounds.

I believe that every person who begins this journey of faith, with all of the tentativeness and hesitation and fear and hope that are a part of that journey, will have an experience that parallels mine. Let's face it, prayer begins with many half-solved questions, mixed together with early hopes and partial evidences. But as we progress, the evidences of God's goodness and faithfulness become surer and stronger, until they become assurances of our profound friendship with him. And as we grow in that assurance, our prayers grow in depth and joyousness—this is the best proof of all.

7

The Crisis of Faith: A Case Study in the Book of Job

For me, over the years prayer has been a most important part of my daily routine, especially at meals and in the morning and evening. But at two other times I respond spontaneously in prayer: when a special joy breaks in upon my loved ones or upon me, or when I or someone I especially know and love is hurting.

Most people experience this, and that is understandable, because at such moments we must not attempt to live alone. In fact, prayer is the most profound of all relational moments, even if we do not feel immediate relational benefits.

A Victim of Disaster

The Old Testament Book of Job tells the story of a man caught in the grip of a lonely crisis, and it documents in living color the impact of that crisis upon Job and the people in his life. While at first we might not understand it this way, the Book of Job is at its center about the most fundamental meanings of prayer.

Without doing a thorough commentary on this unique part of Scripture, we will focus in briefly on the contents as it relates to the message God gives us about prayer. Job doesn't start out with the prayer theme. Rather it begins by recounting dialogue between God and Satan. The Lord asks Satan:

> "Where have you come from?" Satan answered the Lord, "From going to and fro on the earth, and from walking up and down on it." The Lord said to Satan, "Have you considered my servant Job? There is no one like him on the earth, a blameless and upright man who fears God and turns away from evil." Then Satan answered the Lord, "Does Job fear God for nothing? Have you not put a fence around him and his house and all that he has, on every side? You have blessed the work of his hands, and his possessions have increased in the land. But stretch out your hand now, and touch all that he has, and he will curse you to your face."
>
> Job 1:7–11

As a result of this dialogue, God allows his servant Job to experience intense affliction. Job loses all his livestock, his crops, his land, and his children. But while he suffers the agonies of these losses, we read, "In all this Job did not sin or charge God with wrong-doing"(1:22).

An additional conversation between God and Satan follows, and God releases Satan to afflict Job physically but not at the expense of his life. Next, the writer tells us, "So Satan went out from the presence of the Lord, and inflicted loathsome sores on Job from the sole of his foot to the crown of his head. Job took a potsherd with which to scrape himself, and sat among the ashes" (2:7, 8).

Job's Advisors

The major portion of the Job story follows the intense calamities that strike his life. In these scenes we learn of Job's encounters with people and finally with God. A significant part of these involves dialogue between Job and his wife. A series of conversations also takes place between Job and three friends, who, upon hearing of the cataclysmic disasters that Job has experienced, travel from their homes to commiserate with him.

In her anger at the injustice of Job's suffering, Job's wife suggests that he commit suicide, " '. . . Curse God, and die' " (2:9). But for Job, this is not an option he will accept.

Later, when Job speaks to his friends, they generally seem to agree that he is guilty of sin. He needs to repent, they decide, and the only prayer for a man in his condition is the prayer of grief and total apology, an admission of guilt.

These solutions represent the secular and religious answers to human tragedy. Job's wife offers the secular alternative to trusting God. For her, the reasonable choice and natural instinct when someone experiences pain is to move away from it, and because there is injustice in the suffering, the face-saving answer is to curse the source. Job's friends, representing the voice of religion, suggest that Job should not question God. Rather, he should question only himself in an effort to discover what mistakes he had made that brought on the tragic reversal in his fortunes.

Instead of caving in to either suggestion, Job chooses a third way, demanding an audience with God, " 'But I would speak to the Almighty, and I desire to argue my case with God' " (13:3). With these words, Job goes to the very heart of the human search for a way to cope with suffering. Because of Job's insistence and lonely persistence, the message of this story resonates at a profound level with the soul of every person who searches for God and for a way to honestly pray to him.

As we shall see, almost every religious argument made concerning suffering and the ways of prayer is discussed at length by Job's friends. Certainly their arguments are not thoughtless or shallow. In his commentary on the Book of Job, Francis Andersen offers this conclusion about their religious arguments, "What makes this collision of minds so dramatic is the soundness of their views and the cogency of their arguments. The author of the Book of Job has not set up men of straw against Job."[1] While there is cogency at one shallow level, a profound wrongness exists at a deep level, as we will discover in the climactic ending of the story.

The encounters we have in Job provide several cogent ways of understanding human crisis. Some have suggested that this is one reason Job is such an obscure figure in biblical and Jewish history. We know virtually nothing about him—we're only told that he lived somewhere east of the Jordan River. In this rather odd way Job becomes like every other human being who suffers or has felt wronged by disaster. All who hurt feel the same sense of aloneness, and consequently those who suffer relate to everyone else who shares their situation. We all feel the need to pray, but a dryness may fill our mouths when we try to say the words. We relate to Job as he sits in ashes, while his wife and friends attempt to advise him without really helping. Instinctively we understand Job's aloneness during his time of suffering.

The Ingredients of Job's Crisis

There are three ingredients to Job's crisis.

1. The physical and interpersonal suffering, related in the opening words of the story, including the loss of property and his children. This stands as a backdrop to everything else.
2. The crisis instigated by the counsel of Job's wife.
3. Job's confrontation of the crisis, brought on by the counsel he receives from his friends.

The last two crises I will describe as being related to Job's bafflement toward himself and toward God, and these dominate most of the Book of Job—thirty-eight of the forty-two chapters.

In spite of the counsel from Job's wife, he at no time contemplates suicide as the best out for his trouble. When she suggests that he curse God and die, she is angry at God, saying, in effect, "Job, why don't you reject this life? Go out of life in a show of justifiable rage; shake your fist at God and die."

Mrs. Job is like the wife Diffidence, in John Bunyan's *Pilgrim's Progress*. She is the queen in the Castle of Giant Despair, and through her husband, the Giant, she urges Christian and Hopeful to kill themselves, because they are imprisoned there. Fortunately, Christian and Hopeful reject her advice and in the nick of time find the key called the promise of God. With that key they open the castle doors.

Once Job completely rejects his wife's counsel, the rest

of the story centers on the dialogue between Job and his pious friends.

Eliphaz, Bildad, and Zophar. The writer of this ancient story introduces Job's friends by describing how each of them comes together from their respective homes and travels across long miles so they might "console and comfort him." But when they see their friend from a distance, his appearance is so changed that they don't recognize him, ". . . and they raised their voices and wept aloud; they tore their robes and threw dust in the air upon their heads." Then, "They sat with him on the ground seven days and seven nights, and no one spoke a word to him, for they saw that his suffering was very great" (2:11–13).

Job finally broke the week-long period of sympathetic silence when in his agony he "cursed the day of his birth" (3:1). The whole third chapter of this remarkable book is devoted to Job's speech of desperation.

In response to Job's litany of misery, Eliphaz the Temanite launches into a lengthy speech. He begins by telling Job what a fine person he is and how he has accomplished so much good (4:1–6). But after that introductory compliment, Eliphaz gets to the point he wants to make—only sinful people suffer. In effect, Eliphaz says, "Only evil people suffer as badly as you are now. So, come on, Job, what evil have you committed that has produced your suffering?" (4–5).

Following Job's heartrending response to Eliphaz, Bildad the Shuhite picks up on the argument, " 'If you will seek God and make supplication to the Almighty, if you are pure and upright, surely then he [God] will rouse himself for you and restore you to your rightful place' " (8:5, 6).

The dialogue continues as Job agrees that people who are pure will be acceptable to God. But then he asks, " 'How can a mortal be just before God?' " (9:2). Then in desperation he adds, " 'Though I am innocent, I cannot answer him [God]; I must appeal for mercy to my accuser' " (9:15). The rest of Job's speech reflects the intensity of his doom and gloom: " 'I loathe my life; . . . I will speak in the bitterness of my soul. . . . Your hands fashioned and made me; and now you turn and destroy me. . . . I am filled with disgrace. . . . Why did you bring me forth from the womb? Would that I had died before any eye had seen me' " (10:1, 8, 15, 18).

Following Job's lengthy lament, the third friend, Zophar the Naamathite, moves into the center of the scene (Job 11) as he rephrases the central argument. In effect he says, "Your punishment is mild compared to the wrong you must have done. Repent, Job, because, take it from me, I have seen people suffer, and you are not yet suffering anything compared to them." To pick up on a modern-day expression, "With friends like that, Job certainly didn't need any enemies!"

Zophar's bitter counsel prompts Job to make what becomes his central prayer request: " 'What you know, I also know; I am not inferior to you. But I would speak to the Almighty, and I desire to argue my case with God. As for you, you whitewash with lies; worthless physicians are you all' " (Job 13:2–4 RSV). Job makes it clear now; he wants to talk directly with God.

It will be a while before Job gets his wish. In the meantime, Eliphaz gets into the conversation again, and Job makes a response that in turn angers Bildad. In effect Bildad says to Job, "You speak like one who doesn't know God." Broken down into today's language, Bildad said,

"You must not be a Christian, or you wouldn't talk that way."

Job's Prayer of Faith. Bildad's words set up some of the most magnificent lines in the Book of Job:

"O that my words were written down!
O that they were inscribed in a book!
O that with an iron pen and with lead
they were engraved on a rock forever!
For I know that my Redeemer lives,
and that at the last he will stand upon the earth;
and after my skin has been thus destroyed,
then in my flesh I shall see God."

19:23–26

In the middle of Job's anguish he speaks this incredible prayer of faith. Job has arrived at an important decision—in the midst of his confused feelings and suffering he *will* trust in God. This prayer in no way minimizes his confusion or the reality of his suffering. But he firmly grasps the profound conviction that God is his Redeemer and that he lives in spite of Job's suffering and confusion.

Only the Guilty Suffer. Following Job's marvelous statement of faith, Zophar returns to the conversation and says in effect, "I feel insulted by you, Job. Don't you know that guilty people like you are going to experience intense judgment?"

Job counters this kind of reasoning with the statement that it is the just who suffer and the wicked who prosper. This same bold line of reasoning has been amplified by many of Israel's prophets. Jeremiah prayed, "You will be in the right, O Lord, when I lay charges against you; but let me put my case to you. Why does the way of the guilty prosper? Why do all who are treacherous thrive?" (Jeremiah 12:1). That is indeed the cry of history. The just and righteous don't always flourish, and the wicked are not always punished—at least in our lifetimes.

The dialogue continues as Eliphaz launches one final assault against Job in an effort to prove his point, " 'Is not your wickedness great? There is no end to your iniquities' " (Job 22:5). Job's friends are persistent—because his suffering is so great he must be terribly wicked! Such being the case, Eliphaz tells Job, " 'Agree with God, and be at peace; in this way good will come to you' " (22:21).

Job Seeks to Argue His Case Before God. But Job remains resolute. Almost as if he didn't even hear Eliphaz, he prays:

> "Today also my complaint is bitter;
> his hand is heavy despite my groaning.
> Oh, that I knew where I might find him,
> that I might come even to his dwelling!
> I would lay my case before him,
> and fill my mouth with arguments."
> 23:2–4

Once again Job's request is clear and insistent. There is only one answer to his dilemma; he wants to argue his case before God face-to-face. He prays here as if God was his Friend—one who understands his need. "Job rejects the secular solution to holiness. He will not curse God.

He rejects the religious solution to his problem. He will not curse himself. He chooses a third way. He would argue with God." (Jen Palmer, student paper written at Stamford University.)

Now, as we have probed at the meaning behind this remarkable old book, we can begin to understand why it gives us such a splendid case study of the dynamics of prayer. Here Job asks for the right to pray, and for him prayer is fundamentally an encounter between an ordinary person and the Lord who hears. For Job, prayer is not easy, and he struggles to find God. Nevertheless, he reaches out almost frantically to the Lord. In his distress he isn't sure the Lord is his friend, but Job trusts him enough to want to argue with him.

On and on the dialogue goes between Job and his friends. Finally Bildad comes up with the harshest of all speeches as he concludes that Job will never find God and be in a right relationship with him. Bildad's skepticism and cynicism come through in these words, " 'How then can a mortal be righteous before God? How can one born of woman be pure? If even the moon is not bright, and the stars are not pure in his sight, how much less a mortal, who is a maggot, and a human being, who is a worm!' " (25:4–6).

How often have you heard someone say, "I feel like a worm"? It isn't true now any more than it was true in Job's day. There is, of course, a vast contrast between ourselves and God. Yes, any righteousness we might have counts for little in the bright light of God's truth. But we are not maggots or worms in God's sight. He loves us even though we are wayward; our lostness does not minimize our worth.

After these harsh statements by Bildad, Job launches into the longest speech in the entire book (26–31). Once again Job insists that he will accept justice only from God, not from his counselors and friends, as he belabors his case. Finally, silence prevails.

At that point a new voice is heard. Evidently, "Elihu, son of Barachel the Buzite, of the family of Ram" had been a silent onlooker and listener. The writer tells us that Elihu "was angry at Job because he justified himself rather than God; he was angry also at Job's three friends because they had found no answer, though they had declared Job to be in the wrong" (32:2, 3).

In his anger Elihu denounces all of the older men, but as we listen to him we discover that he has nothing new to add to the dialogue. It is just more of the same dreary rehash that has polluted the atmosphere throughout the lengthy discussion (32–37). After Elihu has gone on at considerable length, the Lord moves into the scene. Job has been wanting to find God, now God finds him: "Then the Lord answered Job out of the whirlwind: 'Who is this that darkens counsel by words without knowledge? Gird up your loins like a man, I will question you, and you shall declare to me' " (38:1–3). Then follows God's magnificent challenge to Job (38–41).

Earlier I referred to Job's crisis of bafflement, in which he clung tenaciously to his relationship with God, in spite of his tragic circumstances, his own questions, and the counsel of his wife and friends. Through all of this Job simply held on—his integrity intact even though he had no visible support. What an amazing display of raw faith!

Faith in Action

Karl Barth, one of our century's greatest theologians, gave this amazing definition of faith, which helps me to understand Job just a little bit: "Faith occurs when I hold fast to Christ in spite of all that contradicts faith."[2] The first time I read that sentence I thought, *Barth, you must be wrong. You meant to say that faith occurs when I hold fast to Christ because of all the encouragement I receive from the church, from the witness of my friends, and from all of the biblical authorities.* But that isn't what Karl Barth wrote, and after reading the Book of Job I believe that Barth was right. Faith is the experience that occurs when we hold fast to Christ in spite of the bad advice we receive from friends, and faith enables us to pray when everyone tells us that prayer has no value.

Now, that isn't to say that we always receive bad advice in the course of our Christian walk. And how thankful we can be for the faithfulness of the church, for without it we wouldn't have our Bible, and we would not have heard the good news. However, if we are to have faith in Jesus Christ, we must still have it in spite of the church as much as because of it.

People are sorely misguided who insist they cannot have faith in Christ because of a bad parent or an inept Sunday-school teacher. Remember, we are to hold fast to Christ *in spite* of all that seems to contradict that faith in his faithfulness. Authentic faith is bold, and when we dare to pray, we do so with confidence in the goodness and trustworthiness of Jesus Christ.

This is precisely why the Book of Job is so profoundly messianic. In his heartbreaking distress Job is deeply disappointed by his wife and his pious friends. In his desperation he cries out for a meeting—a conversation—with God. Nothing else matters. He must meet the Lord God himself. Only God can resolve the baffling questions of life. The grand surprise in Job's story is that God grants his request—he answered Job's prayer!

Job gives us a clear message—when for whatever reason, suffering and hard times or any other crisis of faith confronts us, we are to cling tenaciously to the faithfulness and love of God, in spite of everything that seems to contradict it. Indeed, contradictions are a part of life. While we cannot resolve every thoughtful or troubling question that plagues us, we can call out to God.

Prayer is that "call to God" in which we blurt out our deepest feelings. In it we ask our most difficult and perplexing questions and express our most painful aloneness. Then we, like Job, experience the electrifying awareness that the God of our prayers is our Friend.

8

Surprised by Hope: Job, a Book of Prayer

When Bad Things Happen to Good People, a book by Harold Kushner, wrestles with the problem of human suffering. While I don't go along with the main thesis of the book, I do believe he offers some intriguing insights to the Job story.

Kushner reasons that Job's friends and advisors had developed a worldview in which God is good and good things happen to good people. Consequently, when bad things happen to people, it must be because they themselves are bad. This explains their counsel to Job, which said in effect, "Job, just admit how bad you are. Then possibly God will help you, because God is good."

With regard to Job's worldview, Kushner makes the following comment: "Job for his part is unwilling to hold the world together theologically by admitting that he is the villain . . . He is not prepared to lie to save God's reputation."[1] I believe this is correct, because Job, on one side of this dramatic equation, refuses to curse God and die. On the other side of this equation *he refuses to curse himself.* Instead, as we have seen in our overview of the Book of Job, he holds out for a personal confrontation with God himself. Now, as we come at Job's story from a slightly different perspective, we will gain further insight into our discussion on prayer.

As Job repeatedly determines to put his case only before God, it becomes clear that he regards God as the final authority; and he most certainly isn't interested in consulting with Satan, even though he caused Job's trouble. Job knows full well that any and all other powers in heaven or earth are secondary, and he is only interested in talking to the true source of his crisis, who is also his only true source of hope.

God Takes Over

As we have already discovered, some intriguing surprises surface toward the end of Job's story. At the beginning of chapter 38, God interrupted the lengthy speech of young Elihu. Most certainly, Elihu comes across as the most self-righteous of Job's friends. I can't help but wonder if the Lord's interruption at this point signals that the pious advice of Job's friends, who had attempted so carefully to protect God's honor and privilege, bored him. So with exciting abruptness God takes over and speaks directly to Job. God's dialogue with Job dominates the rest of the story.

As I reflect on this in my imagination, I can envision a courtroom scene in which the arguments of the prosecution and defense attorneys grind on endlessly and with boring monotony and detail. Finally, the presiding judge interrupts the proceedings and says, "I've heard enough.

The court is now ready to announce its decision." Such a moment of surprise and tension would be likely to cause consternation, as there were more witnesses to testify. But the judge had heard enough and had formulated his decision.

Five Surprises

God's Response. Now, God has interrupted and moved in. He is prepared to act. And the first surprise for us in this encounter between God and Job is that God doesn't answer the two questions on everyone's mind: *Why is Job suffering?* and, *What must he do to make the suffering stop?* These were key questions for Job, and they are for us, in our times of pain and suffering. But God remains silent on them.

The important thing, though, is that God does respond to Job's most urgent prayer. Four significant things happen in the divine encounter between God and Job. First, though we might miss it unless we are aware of certain customs in ancient Israel, God tells Job to stand up like a man and talk to him. Remember, Job is afflicted with boils, and in those days such a disorder was a symptom of a systemic disease that demanded social isolation. This is why Job had set himself apart in sackcloth and ashes. He was an unclean, repelling sight. But Job's condition neither embarrasses nor repels God, and twice he tells Job to stand up like a man and talk to him (Job 38:3; 40:7).

The Grand Tour. The second surprise in the encounter is the content of the conversation that now takes place. In effect, God takes Job on a grand tour of the created order:

"Where were you when I laid the foundation of the
earth?
Tell me, if you have understanding.
Who determined its measurements—surely you know!
Or who stretched the line upon it?
On what were its bases sunk,
or who laid its cornerstone
when the morning stars sang together
and all the heavenly beings shouted for joy?
Or who shut in the sea with doors
when it burst out from the womb?—
when I made the clouds its garment,
and thick darkness its swaddling band,
and prescribed bounds for it. . . ."

38:4–10

What a vivid picture God presents as the Creator himself takes Job on an expansive journey through what he has made! Job and his heavenly Guide journey from the beginning places of the earth's foundation, to the establishment of the ocean and its boundaries, to the sky, the stars, and the animal kingdom. God shows off all of these wonders to his sickly friend.

I don't know about you, but here an amazing incongruity strikes me. Open wounds and boils cover Job's body; he has finally received his request to meet God, and Job is going to lay out his case. But before he even has a chance to speak, God takes him on this journey. It seems strange and quite inappropriate, until we can understand what is happening to Job in the psychological and spiritual core of his human nature in the presence of God.

I recall my years as a seminary student at Princeton, from 1953–1956. Since my family was on the West Coast, our communication was primarily through the mail. Phone rates for long distance were much higher then, and as a result I think I made only three or four long-distance calls home during those three years.

My father's brother lived in Connecticut, and I often spent holidays with him and my grandmother while I was at Princeton. My uncle loved to talk on the phone, and on every visit, he would say, "Well, let's call the folks." It seemed to me then that he had no concept of time or of the cost of his calls.

His typical conversation with my father went something like this, "Hello, Ward! I'm having a terrible time with my string beans. I've got the crook-neck squash in, and they're doing well, but the zucchinis aren't like last year. I've got butternut squash coming out of my ears. Incidentally, there's a lot of crabgrass in my front lawn, and I don't know what to do about it. And the Hawthorn roses are taking over the west wall. Oh, by the way, I heard Dr. Peale last Sunday when I was in New York. . . ."

While I didn't appreciate it then, I now realize that this is the right way to visit over the telephone. This is the best way to get inside each other's lives—by recounting the little things, the apparent trivia, as though you were sitting together visiting on the front porch.

Now, God does precisely that with Job. As I read this part of the story, I see God talking with a friend. In effect, he says, "Job, stand up on your feet like a man. I'm going to show you around this world of mine. Look over there at the sun. Isn't that marvelous? And look at the sky today. Did you see Orion and the other constellations? How about Planet Earth? The sea, for instance. Isn't it amazing how I set up all of the boundaries to hold the sea in? Incidentally, I'm especially proud of the animals I created. Look at that hippopotamus. Isn't he something? There is Leviathan in the ocean. He's giving me some trouble, but I can control him. . . ."

I see that as the inner mood of the whole dialogue. Many readers of the Book of Job at first feel disappointment that God doesn't do and say more—at least address the painful issues that plague the minds of Job and his friends. But they fail to realize that God is doing something very significant here as he takes Job on a journey, as one friend would another.

We must not wrongly interpret the interrogative portions of this dialogue as God says, " 'Where were you when I created? . . . Tell me if you understand. . . . Surely you know. . . .' " I don't agree with some interpreters' suggestion that God was trying to humiliate Job. Certainly, further humiliation is not what Job needs. We also know from the context of these sentences that this is not God's intention, because in the end the Lord commends Job in front of his stern and unbending spiritual friends. Job is the one who was right; his friends were wrong.

We know in moving on through the story that Job does repent before the Lord, but his repentance is caused by the fact that he has seen the Lord, not because the Lord or circumstances humiliated him. This is the way the Lord Jesus draws us toward repentance. We see his grace, his love, and his truth, and then we recognize our profound need of his wholeness and forgiveness. This happened to the jailer at the prison in Philippi. Based on the marvelous witness of Paul and Silas, the jailer asked, " '. . . Sirs, what must I do to be saved?' " (Acts 16:30). These words came from a man who experienced generous love—not a belittled and humiliated man.

Job Is Satisfied. There are three more surprises in the encounter between God and Job. At the conclusion of God's message for Job, we discover that while at first glance God doesn't seem to answer all of his questions, Job is completely satisfied. Let's take a look at what Job says to God:

> "I know that you can do all things, and that no purpose of yours can be thwarted. 'Who is this that hides counsel without knowledge?' Therefore I have uttered what I did not understand, things too wonderful for me, which I did not know. 'Hear, and I will speak; I will question you, and you declare to me.' I had heard of you by the hearing of the ear, but now my eye sees you.' "
>
> Job 42:2–5

The final part of Job's reply to God is mistranslated in our version where it reads, ". . . therefore I *despise* myself, and *repent* in dust and ashes" (42:6, *italics mine*). The words "despise" and "repent" have much deeper significance in the anicent Hebrew. Probably a better translation is the same idea present in the Book of Acts when Peter preached his sermon on the Day of Pentecost. At the conclusion of the sermon, Luke writes, ". . . they were cut to the heart . . ." (Acts 2:37). What Job says here could be translated, "I have been cut to the heart and have found myself now that I have you."

This is similar to what happened to Isaiah when he met the Lord, and cried, " '*Woe is me!* I am lost, for I am a man of unclean lips . . .' " (Isaiah 6:5, *italics mine*). When he realizes he has met the Christ, Peter exclaims, " 'Go away from me, Lord, for I am a sinful man!' " (Luke 5:8). Both Isaiah and Peter were "cut to the heart."

For Job, though, there is a shock of recognition as he

sees God and as he sees himself. Job is satisfied; he has met the Lord. But even more profoundly, the Lord has met Job and shown himself to him.

God Honors Job for Being Truthful. The next surprise comes in God's statement to Eliphaz, ". . . 'My wrath is kindled against you, and against your two friends; for you have not spoken of me what is right, as my servant Job has' " (Job 42:7). Here God honors Job as a faithful servant who has spoken the truth. By contrast, Job's three friends have said things that were true in some instances; but when put together, they were false. Each of us needs to explore and understand this important principle. Many people who are participants in a confrontation will say something to another person that may be true, when taken by itself, yet it is false when seen in its total context. Many of the hurtful statements we throw at one another have this apparently righteous content, from our "superior" point of view.

The Book of Job helps me realize just how pastorally complicated it is to be a counselor and friend to the people around me. I used to think that the only test of communication was "Is it true?" But now I know it just isn't that simple. For example, when the Van Damm family, in Amsterdam, heard a knock on their door in 1944 and opened it, a member of the German Gestapo confronted them: "We've heard that there is a Jewish family in your house. Have you hidden a Jewish family?"

The truth was, at that very moment the family of Anne Frank was hidden in an upstairs secret compartment of the house. The Gestapo questions posed a dilemma for the Van Damm family. Should they simply tell the truth? As moral people, should they say, "Yes, there is a Jewish family hidden upstairs"?

On the surface, that affirmative answer was true, but it would have been false on a deeper level, because the evil intention of the occupation police force had to be weighed upon a larger biblical and ethical balance scale. Poet William Blake wrestled with this same idea when he wrote, "A truth that's told with bad intent beats all the lies you can invent."

An additional fact emerges in the concluding drama of the Job story as we catch the truth that the one who was most afflicted had become in the end the one with the deepest insight. Job, who on the surface seemed to have reason to be the most angry at God, had in fact spoken the greatest truth about God. This comes through clearly in the Lord's conversation with Eliphaz.

In the Job story it isn't the people who appear to be the best off and who seem to have the best relationship with God who most often speak the truth. This fact can awaken a new awareness to our own evaluations of others. We must remain open to the idea that the person who is unable to pray easily, who is unable to readily express thanks to God, or who seems to be troubled by God may in fact be expressing the deepest truth about and to God.

The Lord's endorsement of Job should silence once and for all the false disqualifers that a person with problems cannot possibly have truth to share with someone else, that the person in crisis should only receive advice, not give it. Certainly, for those of us who have had our moments of feeling desperately inadequate, this word of the Lord to Job is good news, because in his times of greatest crisis, Job had the word of truth for us.

Job Had Asked the Right Questions. One final surprise appears in the closing words of Job's story. When God told Eliphaz that he was angry with him and his other two friends, because they hadn't spoken the truth, but Job had, it comes through clearly that while God hadn't given Job an answer to his questions, Job had asked the right questions.

What is the meaning for us here? Job didn't get an answer to his question about suffering, but he got something better! Job met God. While he didn't get answers to his deepest questions, he did have a divine encounter with the One to whom we can direct all of our questions.

That is the key point of the entire Book of Job. Many people have suffered in the centuries since Job had his trials, and we must always question the injustices that prevail in our world, but in reality no answers really satisfy us. Instead, the Bible gives us something far better as it presents the Person who suffers with us. In this way, Job received a down payment of the deeper answer that was to come centuries later—the One who would identify totally with Job.

All this leads me to say that I believe the Book of Job is the most messianic of all the Old Testament books. At the same time, it is the most profound of the prayer books, because it is the story of a person who will not be satisfied with anything less than a personal encounter with God. Job the man and Job the book invite all who read the story into an experience of vital prayer. Job is met by God, and he meets God—his Friend. This ancient meeting prepares each of us who read the story of that encounter to discover that Job's deepest yearning will be fulfilled in Jesus of Nazareth, the One who will suffer even more than Job did.

That is the power of prayer! Saint Paul described this deeper meaning when he wrote to the Christians in Philippi:

> Let the same mind be in you that was in Christ Jesus, who, though he was in the form of God, did not regard equality with God as something to be exploited, but emptied himself, taking the form of a slave, being born in human likeness. And being found in human form, he humbled himself and became obedient to the point of death—even death on a cross.
>
> Philippians 2:5–8

Jesus here identified with people even to death by Roman crucifixion. This is the reason why Jesus is the One who is most able to identify with us. We don't have an answer to the problem of suffering and evil, but we have Jesus Christ, who suffered for and with us. We have the Man for the crisis, and Job experienced the beginnings of that hope.

The Happy Ending

The happy ending of the Book of Job (42:10–17) displeases some Bible interpreters. Here we read that the Lord restored Job's fortunes. In fact, he received twice as much as he had before. The writer adds, "The Lord blessed the latter days of Job more than his beginning; and he had fourteen thousand sheep, six thousand camels, a thousand yoke of oxen, and a thousand donkeys. He also had seven sons and three daughters" (42:12, 13).

Professor Francis Andersen observes about the conclusion of the Job story:

> Some scholars have complained that the story is ruined by the happy ending. As if the author had slipped back into the crude theology of punishments and rewards which it was his aim in the discourse to

> discredit. . . . These gifts at the end are gestures of grace, not rewards of virtue. It is an artistic, indeed theological fitness, if not necessity, that Job's vindication be not just a personal and hidden reconciliation with God in the secret of his soul, but also visible, material, historical in terms of his life as man. It was already a kind of resurrection in the flesh as much as the Old Testament could know. Job's complete vindication had to wait until the resurrection of Lazarus and of a greater than Lazarus.[2]

At this point in my own Christian pilgrimage I am convinced that from God Job received personal confirmation of what Saint Paul would later call grace: the surprise gift of love that assures us of God's love. To recognize this is to confront the very core of what prayer is all about.

Prayer is not power; it is our relationship with the Friend who has all power. This relationship has more importance than answers to our particular questions. Questions and answers are temporary at best; the relationship is permanent. This does not downgrade our questions about life, but it puts them into the larger and more lasting context of the goodness and faithfulness of God.

Part III

Praying in Jesus' Name

9

Teach Us to Pray

Prayer is for amateurs; it is not an art form that has more power in it if the pray-er learns and masters certain secrets. It does not require ritual or religious skill, because it is the language of relationship between ordinary human beings and the Lord of Life.

The sacred Scriptures of the Old Testament invite us to pray: "Come now, let us argue it out, says the Lord . . ." (Isaiah 1:18). Jesus Christ offers the same invitation to the human family: " 'Ask and it will be given you; search, and you will find; knock and the door will be opened for you' " (Matthew 7:7).

The Model Prayer

In the New Testament we find the prayer Jesus taught his followers for their daily use (Matthew 6:9–13). Throughout the history of Christendom it has remained a vital prayer–song for believers, much used in Christian worship. Many who have just entered the journey of faith have used this prayer as a first expression of trust.

We who live in the twentieth century have what is commonly called the Lord's Prayer because of the witness of the New Testament Gospels of Matthew and Luke. Before giving this prayer to his first disciples, Jesus spoke a warning and a promise. He bluntly warned his disciples to say what they meant, when they prayed, and to say it simply, with a few words. He also told them God would hear. Such a warning and promise assure that our heavenly Father knows us well.

All Jesus' teaching about prayer made it clear that God isn't honored by senseless and monotonous repetition. We don't need to remind God of his existence and of his greatness. Nor do we need to repeat our requests obsessively. The God who knows us well knows our needs, too.

The theological and psychological implications of Jesus' teaching about prayer are very important for us today. He has shown us that neither emotional nor intellectual intensity guarantees truth. Voluminous words and passionate feeling are not tests of reality. On one occasion Martin Luther said our prayers should be "brief, frequent, and intense." Centuries before the great Reformer spoke those words of wisdom, Jesus gave us his magnificent model prayer: the Lord's Prayer.

The writer of Matthew's Gospel gives us these words of Jesus:

> "When you are praying, do not heap up empty phrases as the Gentiles do; for they think that they will be heard because of their many words. Do not be

like them, for your Father knows what you need before you ask him.

"Pray then in this way:

Our Father in heaven,
hallowed [central] be your name.
Your kingdom come,
Your will be done,
on earth as it is in heaven.
Give us this day our daily bread.
And forgive us our debts,
as we also have forgiven our debtors.
And do not bring us to the time of trial,
but rescue us from the evil one."

Matthew 6:7–13

The prayer is brief, very personal, but not private or singular. For example, you and I can sit or kneel side by side, with each of us praying the same words—it is my prayer, but at the same time it is yours. These words of Jesus have an expansive and universal ring to them, yet they honor human uniqueness and individuality. At the same time this simple prayer stands in stark contrast to the pattern prevalent in the first-century Roman and Greek world.

The Pagan View of Prayer

Jesus had already warned his disciples to avoid "empty phrases" and "many words," because of the confusing effect of the religious intoxication of the time. There was a widespread belief in many different gods and goddesses, along with, in certain cities of the empire, the mandated worship of the Roman emperors. Greek and Roman mythology was very complex and chaotic.

The history of the city of Pergamum illustrates this kind of religious complexity. Pergamum was a beautiful Greek city, in the region of Mysia, in western Asia Minor, a thriving first-century metropolis. In addition to several temples set apart for emperor worship, it had temples to Zeus; to Asclepius, the Greek god of healing; to Athena; and to Dionysus. The citizens of Pergamum were expected to worship at all of these.

In the Book of Revelation John refers to Pergamum as the place "where Satan's throne is," possibly because it was one of the oldest and most prominent centers of Roman emperor worship. Archaeological excavations of the site give us a detailed account of the complex worship patterns of the pagan religions that thrived in the first century. Roman historian Publius Tacitus (A.D. 55–120) admitted candidly that many first-century Romans and Greeks were attracted to the Jewish religion because of its lack of excessive language, shrines, and complex rituals.

However, Tacitus himself preferred the drama and showy spectacle of the Greco-Roman cultic religions; he considered the Jewish faith "mean and tastless" because of the absence of beautiful statues and stately shrines. But the simplicity of the Jewish faith helped many men and women of the first century to ask the important questions about ultimate reality, and in the synagogue they furthered their search. There they discovered the Old Testament writings—the law, prophets, and songs that prepared many of these searchers for the dramatic confrontation with Jesus of Nazareth.

The prayers in the Jewish Scriptures were simple and straightforward, unlike the incantations made at the temple of Bacchus, Apollo, or Eleusis. Jewish prayers held no magic terms, like the word *abracadabra,* which was found in a first-century papyrus. No, the law, the Psalms—prayer–songs—and prophetic writings of sacred Scripture stood out in sharp contrast to the prayers and poems of the first-century pagan Mediterranean religions. Old Testament prayers and prayer–songs are delightfully uncomplicated and nonrepetitious, with no promise of magical powers. Rather, they are the language of dialogue and friendship.

Our New Testament Scriptures provide a fascinating clue concerning the contrast between pagan and Christian prayers. In the Book of Acts Luke vividly describes a scene in Ephesus, when companions of the Apostle Paul became victims of pagan religious frenzy. It seems the Christian message they had preached there interfered with the trade of those who made silver images of Diana (Artemis), the fertility goddess whose temple was one of the seven wonders of the ancient world and a great tourist attraction.

The indignant silversmiths instigated a riot in the massive amphitheater for which Ephesus was famous. Almost thirty thousand people were whipped up into a religious frenzy as "for about two hours all of them shouted in unison, 'Great is Artemis of the Ephesians!' " (Acts 19:28–35). Imagine! For two hours they chanted, "Great is Artemis of the Ephesians!" This kind of prayer was hardly the language of friendship or dialogue. They couldn't think of anything else to say.

A Shocking Salutation

Understanding the pagan religious mind-set in the first century and the Jewish attitude toward prayer and religious practices can help us in our own prayer pilgrimage. When Jesus told his Jewish followers to pray, "Our Father," they would have been shocked at the use of his word *Father*. First-century Judaism's Pharisaic movement held to a very narrow interpretation of the third commandment, "You shall not make wrongful use of the name of the Lord your God, for the Lord will not acquit anyone who misuses his name" (Exodus 20:7). The Pharisees refused to use the name for God, *Yahweh,* but instead held to indirect references as signs of awe and reverence.

Consequently, our Lord's informality and intimacy in using "Our Father" represented a drastic departure from what was accepted at the time. But Jesus wanted his followers in all of time to understand that our prayers are directed to the Lord who knows who we are and who knows our needs. In addition, we are to pray to God in language that acknowledges who he is—our godly Parent, our Father.

It is helpful for us to understand, too, that prayer as practiced by the Jewish people in the first century was very "kingdom oriented." The Talmud went so far as to assert, "That prayer in which there is no mention of the kingdom of God is not a prayer." In other words, instead of being personal and warm, prayer had become institutionalized.

The discovery and translation of the Dead Sea Scrolls underscores this fact. The scrolls include many prayers of this period. Noted for their lack of warmth, they were directed primarily toward technical concerns of the community. Most of these community prayers relate to war or victory or national success. One notable exception to this pattern is found in the first century *Kaddish*. It is very personal and much like the Our Father prayer:

May His great name be magnified and sanctified
in the world which he has created according to his will. May his
sovereignty reign in your life
and in your days, and in the life of all the house of Israel,
speedily and at a near time.
And say ye amen.

The word *kingdom* is an important one in the world of both the Old and New Testaments. In reality, as it is used in our Bible, it is a relationship word, not a geographical or political one. Rarely does the Old Testament Hebrew word for "kingdom" take on a spatial sense, because God's reign is neither spatial nor static. Rather, *kingdom* is a dynamic idea; it denotes the reign of God in action.

The Intimate Language of Relationship

While the first-century Jews were not accustomed to using the intimate and relational term *Father* in their prayers, in using it, Jesus looked back to an earlier ancient tradition that predated by centuries this highly artificial reticence of the Pharisee movement. Even as *Yahweh* is used 5,500 times in the Old Testament, so the word *Father* is commonly used there to describe God's relationship to his people.

The ancient Song of Moses reminded the people of Israel ". . . Is not he [God] your father, who created you, who made you and established you?" (Deuteronomy 32:6). Later both Isaiah and Jeremiah spoke of God as "Father," "For you are our father . . ." (Isaiah 63:16); ". . . And I thought you would call me, My Father, and would not turn from following me" (Jeremiah 3:19). Later the prophet Malachi recorded God's haunting question, "A son honors his father, and servants their master. If then I am a father, where is the honor due me? And if I am a master, where is the respect due me? says the Lord of hosts to you . . ." (1:6). And finally, in the intertestamental Book of Wisdom, probably written sometime in the first century B.C., we find a most important messianic prophecy, "He calls the last end of the righteous happy, and boasts that God is his father" (2:16).

In truth, Jesus fulfilled the expectation of the writer of the Book of Wisdom, and according to the Gospel of John, Jesus claimed this intimate term in the most complete sense. In an argument with the Pharisees, he responded to their question, " 'Where is your Father?' " " 'You know neither me nor my Father. If you knew me, you would know my Father also' " (8:19). According to the Gospel writers, Jesus didn't claim this relationship only for himself—he invited his followers to approach God with the same word.

Finally, in the Garden of Gethsemane, our Lord made use of the even more personal and affectionate Aramaic expression *Abba,* when he prayed, " 'Abba, Father, for you all things are possible; remove this cup from me; yet, not what I want, but what you want' " (Mark 14:36).

The Apostle Paul affirms the same intimate and affectionate term when he wrote the Christians in Rome, ". . . When we cry 'Abba! Father!' it is that very Spirit bearing witness with our spirit that we are children of God" (Romans 8:15, 16). Indeed, Christians in all of time are invited to use these intimate and relational terms in talking to God.

In the opening two words of the Lord's Prayer—"Our Father"—Jesus reestablished the felt sense of closeness to God that was the mark of the prophets and the psalmists but had been suppressed in the life of Israel from the time of the Maccabean revolt onward, especially by the Pharisee movement. This means that from about 156 B.C. to the time of our Lord's ministry the prayers of Israel had become increasingly specialized, formal, and kingdom oriented—less personal and less intimate. Instead of breaking with tradition, Jesus actually turned our eyes upon an even older tradition. It is interesting, isn't it, that what we sometimes think of as a new and fresh personalism is really the exciting return to an ancient friendliness. These first two words of the Lord's Prayer seal that profound, old, personal friendship between God and his people.

10

Thy Kingdom, Lord

I vividly recollect an experience I had during my six years of ministry as a pastor in the Philippines (1964–1970). On a particular afternoon, when I was with a student group at a week-long retreat at Camp John Hay, the United States Air Force Recreational Base, playing with them and my own small children on the beautiful lawns, I heard the sound of jet planes overhead. I looked up and saw the unmistakable jet trails of six B-52 bombers as they streaked across the deep-blue tropical sky. I knew they were on their way to carry out a bombing mission over Vietnam.

When the planes were out of sight and sound, I looked out across the lawns again at our young people, still immersed in their football game. A vast uneasiness and a profound feeling of helplessness clutched at my consciousness as I realized just how impermanent everything is in a world caught in the grips of a regional war fought with devastating weapons. In such uneasy times, would the Philippines escape the havoc of war? Where would the carefree young people out there on that grass field be a year from now? Two years? Five years?

Your Kingdom Come

That afternoon I prayed the prayer our Lord taught his disciples, but the opening sentence became more urgent and important to me than ever before, "Your kingdom come. Your will be done on earth as it is in heaven." Admittedly, the "kingdoms" of our present world are fragile. They shake and tremble and reel under threat of war, the calamities of nature, and all the uncertainties that plague our existence. So it becomes terribly important for our lives to be grounded in *the* certain foundation. How important it is for God's rule and will to be at the foundations of our lives.

After Jesus teaches us to address God as "our Father," he teaches us to acknowledge God's holiness and look for his reign upon our earth. As we have seen, in the New Testament the kingdom of God is relational, not territorial. It is where the King and his subjects—the people of God—are.

By his sovereign decision the King of all creation also created the earth we live on. He sustains it, redeems it, and will fulfill its destiny. Now, in our Lord's Prayer, he invites us to say in effect, "O God, we seek first of all your presence as Lord." Or to put it another way, "O God, grant your reign as the solid ground beneath everything else." It is a prayer for the eternal God—the Alpha and Omega, the beginning and the end—to be the one place, the solid ground, on which we may stand and build our lives.

The Right Place to Begin

At the beginning of my studies of the Lord's Prayer, it seemed to me then that it would make better sense to put this petition at the close of the prayer. There is an eschatological "coming of Christ the King" feeling about the language of the kingdom that would have been, I thought, more psychologically appropriate at the conclusion of a series of practical requests. This aspiration for the Lord of all history would then surround the earthy and urgent requests for survival, forgiveness, and protection from evil.

Now I can see how right it was for Jesus to make this the first request in the prayer, because apart from this foundation—this beginning place—we have no hope or reason to pray. Contrary to my original preferences, as I came to see later, our Lord rightly gave us instructions that before we pray for anything else, we ask, "Your kingdom come. Your will be done, on earth as it is in heaven." We are to pray for God's presence before praying for anything else. This is psychologically and theologically sound. If we are to live and work in relationship with other people and become all that God wants us to be as his creation, our first priority must center on the presence of God as the ground or foundation beneath everything else.

Our Most Profound Anxiety

This persistent worry about "the ground beneath everything"—our foundation—is the most profound anxiety known to humankind. It is amply illustrated by the picture and fear of a little girl who had been lost and had wandered for hours in the park but who was now safe at the park police station. Yet she continues to sob uncontrollably with intense fear because the earth or the foundation beneath her very existence—represented by her mother and father—has been lost.

From all outward appearances, the police station scene is safe. The little girl grips her ice-cream cone, the officers are friendly and solicitous, the TV set is tuned to a children's program. Yet the shudder of paralyzing fear that still grips this little girl stems from a primeval anxiety about "the ground beneath everything."

This fear—this ache—remains as real in these closing years of the twentieth century as it was in the Mediterranean world of the first century. Even though much about our world setting seems impressive and solid, the ache persists in spite of all the human schemes to divert our attention from it. The gnawing fear eats at the very vitals of our existence in spite of our efforts to repress it. Materialism and spiritualism are both in their own ways desperate forms of denial of the real fear. In the words of Blaise Pascal, "We cling . . . but nothing stays for us."

But Jesus Christ taught his hearers—and us—to pray a very basic prayer. In my words, this is what he said, "Before you pray for anything else, pray this, 'O God, grant first of all a solid ground—a firm foundation—beneath everything.' "

I believe the heart of every person who has ever lived cries this, and it is the first request in the Lord's Prayer, "Your kingdom come. . . ." With these words we pray for the foundation that is strong enough to bear the weight of everything—the wars that tear apart families and nations—it is also the prayer for little children lost in the park.

A Certain Basis for Optimism. Before we pray for bread or for forgiveness, we pray that the ground of

God's character and reign will form the foundation beneath our lives. Jesus Christ is not only the Earth's Redeemer; he is the Earth's Sustainer. Consequently, this is our most urgent prayer, because it faces up to the shaking of the foundations. Paul Tillich, the theologian–philosopher, once said, "One may face many things cynically . . . but there is one thing we cannot be cynical about, and that is the shaking of the foundations of everything."

Theologically this means Jesus teaches us to live in what we call the present by the fact that he himself boundaries history at its origin, at its center, and at its end. The Lord's Prayer reaches out to the future, yet is anchored profoundly in the past acts of God and in his faithfulness here and now. Since our Lord invites us to pray this prayer, we have confidence that he will grant it.

Practically this implies that we are given a basis for genuine optimism—for the enduring hope concerning the separate parts of our lives, as well as the ground that is steady beneath everything.

11

One Day at a Time

The second movement of the prayer that Jesus gave us is contained in one simple and short sentence, "Give us this day our daily bread." Here we have the essence of directness and practical immediacy.

The word translated "daily" is from the Greek word *epiousios*. This particular word is found only twice in our New Testament Scriptures—here and in Luke's account of the giving of the prayer (Luke 11:3). This word usage is found in only one other first-century citation—a list of business expenses. Its precise meaning is a bit uncertain; however, perhaps our best clue as to the sense of the word is found in a sentence by the wisdom writer, ". . . give me neither poverty nor riches; feed me with the food that I need" (Proverbs 30:8). This common and earthy request for today's food or for needful food is the sense of the Greek word *epiousios* as found in the first-century expense document.

The majority of linguistic and biblical scholars accept the translation of *epiousios* as "daily," as we have it in our Bibles. Consequently, Jesus here invites us to share with God our Father our concerns for the very earthy, basic aspects of human existence—the physical elements we need for survival. Notice that in this short and simple prayer request Jesus runs counter to the aspirations of two worldviews: the materialistic and the spiritualistic.

The Materialistic Worldview

Materialism is the iron embrace of our world; it describes a life-style in which people gain meaning for life from *material* things. Materialism accepts the fallacy that what we own gives meaning to life. Its philosophy judges people by the size and appearance of their home, the make and horsepower of their automobile, the size of their bank account, and the neighborhood in which they live; and materialism measures people's worth by their vocation, along with country club membership.

By contrast the people of God understand that the material ingredients important and even essential to life are gifts of a God who cares about us and everything involved in making it through each of our twenty-four-hour days. We don't receive meaning from these ingredients or gifts as such—instead our meaning comes from the whole of life as provided by a loving God.

In this petition Jesus places every material experience and possession into a daily context. Each day we need bread, because like every other part of God's creation, bread has its limitations. Food only sustains and nourishes our bodies for a finite time. There is a natural, built-in limitation to every substance, food, or treasure of the earth. The theological implication of these words is that when the meaning of our lives becomes founded on any aspect of God's creation, it is rooted in too small a place. Instead, a larger and more magnificent whole gives meaning to life.

When he makes this petition, Jesus gives meaning to the logical and real need of people to survive physically. Jesus neither discounts nor treats this essential part of our lives with contempt. Rather, he treats it as an ingredient of the whole. Our daily bread, along with the other essentials of our human existence, takes on meaning not of itself but from its Source.

The dangerous flaw of capitalism or communism as an end in itself is in the temptation toward a materialistic devotion to the physical ingredients of life as a whole, instead of devotion to the eternal Source of it all.

In this prayer–petition Jesus puts the physical ingredients of life into a daily context. We need the renewal of food daily, and this daily need is an illustration of the true nature of all that makes up the whole of our physical needs. Each individual part of our physical life is limited and not final in itself—only God stands beyond the boundary of "our daily bread."

Freedom From Material Tyranny

When we truly mean what we say in this second petition of the Lord's Prayer, we are set free from the tyranny of our "daily bread" and of any and all other possessions. Once this happens, we can become stewards of the whole of life, as God has planned. When this prayer becomes the actual conviction of our lives, we are not as possessive and obsessive as before—not as edgy or desperate or superstitious.

Further, we must see that this prayer petition in no way includes a protest against hard work for bread or an argument against responsibility toward our good earth. The awareness of stewardship, which is an ingredient of this prayer petition, increases our respect for "the fruit of the earth," because we see its good origin as a meaningful investment of God's design and intention for the Earth.

The materialist, on the other hand, is tempted toward a careless and presumptuous ownership and even worship of the earth and what it produces. But God created none of the ingredients of the earth for our devotion and worship. For this reason we worship neither "the crocodile nor the sun." Instead we honor this place we call Earth because of its good origin and its goal. We anchor our stewardship in God's ultimate intention for our earth as described by the Apostle Paul in his letter to the Roman Christians, ". . . The creation itself will be set free from its bondage to decay and will obtain the freedom of the glory of the children of God" (8:21). This prayer–petition is a frontal challenge to materialism, because it directs our attention to the spiritual Source of things, great and small—toward the goodness and faithfulness of a friendly God whose loving care is with us always. Nothing else in all of the universe deserves our worship, but everything gains in significance and importance and wonder when God is worshiped!

The Spiritualistic Worldview

Even as this brief prayer sentence offers a challenge to every form of materialism, it comes as an abrupt surprise to a *spiritualistic* worldview. Very likely a pious spiritualist would have composed an entirely different prayer. It could well have gone something like, "O God, help us to have supremacy of spirit over the body so that we will no longer need the daily bread of physical and emotional support from the material world of things and people—to the end that our spirits may soar!"

Many people would prefer a more "spiritual" prayer to the earthy one Jesus gave us. Their reasons would have gone something like this: "Prayer should lift our sights way above crass and earthy concerns." In addition, such pray-ers would consider the word "daily" to be an affront to the spiritual quest of the human spirit. After all, isn't the spiritual goal of the human spirit to avoid—if at all possible—any and every tie to the daily, "ordinary," and limited life so common among "nonspiritual" folks? For the spiritualist, "Give us our daily cake" would be a far better and nobler prayer. After all, ordinary bread, the kind consumed by hungry ordinary people, is so very commonplace!

Interestingly, certain of the early interpreters of the "Our Father" prayer fell into this spiritualistic trap because they felt that "ordinary" bread was too worldly for spiritual folks. Tertullian, Cyprian, and even Augustine were of the opinion that Jesus must have been inviting his disciples to pray for something more than just ordinary bread. Augustine saw this as a prayer for "the invisible bread of the word of God." But Augustine's spiritualizing our prayer for bread misses the point entirely—it certainly doesn't make us more spiritual.

Saint Jerome, another early church father (A.D. 374–420), Christian ascetic, and biblical scholar, advanced this same view in his Latin translation of the Bible, when he translated the word *epiousios,* "supersubstantial." We understand now that there is no basis for this translation, but Jerome, along with Augustine and the others, was swayed by an earnest desire for a "higher" spiritual meaning for a simple sentence. In doing this, they adopted a luxurious rather than a lean interpretation of this petition. In matters like this, the wisest rule for biblical interpretation has always been the guiding principle "lean is better than luxurious."

In this petition of our Lord's Prayer we see that Jesus Christ fully understood both the material and the spiritual quest of people. Certainly we need not play loose with the wording in order for the prayer to be more spiritual and profound; it is already profound in its directness and simplicity.

Some Final Questions

It seems to me at this point that it will be helpful to look at a couple of final questions related to this petition of the prayer: Does our belief that daily life is a gift from God make us less realistic, less creative, and responsible toward ourselves and our earth? Wouldn't we be more creative if we were more autonomous and not so slavishly dependent upon God?

Free to Be Stewards of God's Creation

In response to these questions, I firmly believe that our God-given role as stewards and not owners of any part of the earth is more creative than either the materialistic or the spiritualistic view of life. I also believe that the Bible calls us to a discipleship that involves just the right degree of limitation to prevent us from setting ourselves up as gods; it prevents any part of God's creation from becoming an idol of our affections and/or the specter of our fears.

God, our beloved Father and loving Friend, has set us free from the two equally terrifying bondages of *materialism* and *spiritualism* so that we are free to act and be at work in a healthy relationship with the real world around us. This means that we are free to pray for daily help in our periods of health crisis, while utilizing the latest techniques in medicine. It also means that as we pray for daily food we work hard to support ourselves and our families so that we have food to eat and homes to shelter us. But as we exercise this God-given stewardship we can be under no false illusions about ourselves, as if we were autonomous. This second prayer petition takes us on to a better way of life—a daily way.

12

Forgiveness

Our Lord's Prayer continues with a third petition, " 'And forgive us our debts, as we also have forgiven our debtors.' " Following the conclusion of the prayer itself Jesus expands briefly on this petition as he adds, " 'For if you forgive others their trespasses, your heavenly Father will also forgive you; but if you do not forgive others, neither will your Father forgive your trespasses' "(Matthew 6:14, 15).

This part of the prayer basically assumes that we are all guilty and all need forgiveness. The prayer doesn't read, "And those sinister ones among you who have sinned should pray, 'Forgive us our debts.' " No, Jesus is saying that each one of us is in need of forgiveness.

Forgiveness: A Fundamental Need

Forgiveness is the most fundamental need of people everywhere, and in the sense of this prayer, this is something we cannot do either for ourselves or others. Only what German theologian and World War II martyr Dietrich Bonhoeffer described as "cheap grace" is available to be self-administered and comfortably under our own control. Real forgiveness is an experience of grace, and we are never able to control or personally manage grace.

It is fortunate for us in every way that neither our religious technique nor our desire for power can bring God's forgiveness under our control. We come closest to the heart of the gospel of Jesus Christ at this profound moment in the Lord's Prayer because we are at the place of agreement in which we humbly submit ourselves to the love of God that is able to reconcile us and resolve every estrangement that distorts and confuses our lives. And we ask for God's help for this reconciliation in the simple prayer, " 'forgive us our debts' "—our sins. Jesus Christ himself encourages us to ask for this help, and that makes all the difference in the world.

The Greek word translated "forgive" in this part of the prayer is *aphiemi*. It is both interesting and illuminating to discover that this same Greek word is translated "abandoned" in Revelation 2:4 and "leave" in John 14:27. Paul uses this same word in 1 Corinthians 7:11, where it is translated "divorce." In bringing these various usages together, we see that the literal meaning of the word *aphiemi* is "to leave behind, to cancel, to abandon"—all of which are involved in the word "forgiveness" in the Lord's Prayer. In other words, God leaves behind and cancels our sins.

The word "debts" is an accurate translation of the word used in this part of the prayer (Matthew 6:12), but it is translated "trespasses" in Matthew 6:15. In a practical sense we owe God lives of obedience and righteousness, yet we keep defaulting. Consequently, "debts" becomes a metaphor for "sins"—the word Luke uses in his version of the prayer (Luke 11:4). Combining the Matthew and Luke wording of this petition, we have three different words—"debts," "trespasses," and "sins." Each describes the person who has fallen short in a harmful way, not only hurting the self but others as well.

A Prayer—Not a Bargain

This petition, " 'Forgive us our debts . . . ,' " has two parts; it is a prayer and not a bargain. Notice, it does not say, "Lord, watch how generous we have been toward those who have offended us. Now please be generous toward us in view of these achieved credits that have accumulated to our benefit." Instead, the sense of the prayer goes something like this, "Lord, please grant us forgiveness—something we know about and appreciate from our human experiences with one another—and help us to share the forgiveness we receive with those nearby who need our forgiveness."

In Jesus' explanatory words immediately following the prayer (Matthew 6:14, 15), he gives us the mandate to experience fully the ethical implications of forgiveness: If we forgive, then God has completed forgiveness and its good result in our lives. We don't set the rules, Christ does. This disqualifies the kind of praying we hear all too often, "God, if you'll just get me this job—or resolve the conflict with my parents or rescue me from this crisis—then I'll serve you faithfully and do wonderful things for your kingdom."

This petition of our Lord's Prayer asks for the help of God's grace; it is not an arrangement *quid pro quo*. In an earlier reference we saw how the classical Greek word for pray, *euchomai,* carries within it the sense of "a vow" or even a bargain. But prayer in the Bible is radically different. Both the Old and New Testaments clearly make the point that our prayers to God our Father are not vows or bargains. Rather, prayer brings our whole selves into God's presence.

C. S. Lewis has captured the profound implications of this truth in the way he portrays Aslan's relationship with the children in the seven stories of The Chronicles of Narnia. In *The Magician's Nephew,* Digory discovers the immense creative power of Aslan, the great, golden Lion, Son of the Emperor from Beyond the Sea. But a deep worry rests heavily upon Digory's heart as he remembers the grave illness of his mother, who is back in England, while Digory has been caught up in his wondrous adventures in Narnia. The boy's worry is heightened because he does not understand the mysterious rules of Aslan's Narnia, whereby time spent there does not encroach on time in Digory's real world of England.

Just at that point, Aslan calls to Digory in order to send him on a long and dangerous mission. Lewis narrates this encounter:

> " 'Son of Adam', said Aslan. 'Are you ready. . . ?' 'Yes', said Digory. He had had for a moment some wild idea of saying 'I'll try to help you if you'll promise to help about my mother', but he realized in time that the Lion was not at all the sort of person one could try to make bargains with. But when he had said, 'Yes' . . . a lump came in his throat and tears in his eyes and he blurted out: 'But please, please—won't you—can't you give me something that will cure Mother?' "[1]

That is precisely the Bible's teaching on prayer: We are to blurt out our true feelings, our deepest needs, and bring them to the Lord who has invited us to do that very thing. But prayer is in no sense a bargain. When Digory blurted out his earnest request, it was just that, nothing more and nothing less. His request is in every sense even more daring than a bargain. He is coming into the presence of Aslan with his whole and real self and with his deepest care.

When we pray, we risk ourselves to God, and in that daring experience we made the discovery of his presence and of his care for us and our world. It happens when we dare to blurt out our deepest questions. It happened for Digory in a strange way on that afternoon in Narnia. He looked at the face of Aslan, and he saw a great tear in the eye of the golden Lion.

A New Beginning in Spite of Scars

Several years ago, at a National Youth Worker's Convention, I met a young man who had spent three years of his life in my city, Berkeley, California. During that time he had lived as a nomadic youth on Telegraph Avenue. Toward the end of that period he had met a Christian family from the First Presbyterian Church, where I am now pastor. He told me how this family had befriended him and how, finally, through their witness, he was converted and put his trust in Jesus Christ as Savior and Lord.

His life was radically rearranged as he experienced the healing love of Christ following his conversion. He became reconciled with his parents and returned home to the East Coast. He then finished school, was later married and started his own family. Now, some six years later, he was a highly motivated man in his thirties, a husband and father. But as he concluded his story, he said something that made a deep impression on me, "You know, a large part of those three years that I wandered up and down Telegraph Avenue in Berkeley are just a blur in my memory. I have only shadowy recollections of those years, but I have some scars on my arms that prove I was there."

This young man had experienced a loving and friendly heavenly Father's forgiveness, as Jesus promised in this prayer. That forgiveness didn't mean he could relive those three lost years or that the needle marks from those confused days and nights would disappear. But his past has been resolved and reconciled by the grace of the Savior. He doesn't have the privilege of returning to the past and redoing it. He can't recapture the innocence that preceded his Telegraph Avenue existence, but through his repentance and Christ's forgiveness, he has made a new beginning right in the middle of his life journey.

The promise and the experience of forgiveness are quite different from our early innocence, and certainly Jesus does not offer his disciples a promise of innocence in this prayer; the harm of bad mistakes and poor choices do not disappear completely. Inevitably, scars remain, and missed chances are still missed chances, but through the reconciliation and healing of Christ we are able to make new beginnings. For this radical newness of reconciliation Jesus invites us to pray.

Forgiveness Conditions

Now, we notice conditions in this particular prayer petition. The prayer creates a connection between our experience of forgiveness and our inescapable obligation to the people around us. The second part of this petition has challenged not only the pray-ers of this prayer but those who have attempted to interpret it and understand its full meaning.

As we've seen, following the conclusion of this prayer, Jesus added a sentence that strengthened the importance of the second half of this petition, "For if you forgive others their trespasses, your heavenly Father will also forgive you; but if you do not forgive others, neither will your Father forgive your trespasses" (Matthew 6:14, 15).

It comes through clearly here that Jesus wisely understands that his disciples will not be living in an ideal setting, free from the threat of sin and its harmful consequences. At the same time it is clear that Christian disciples will bear the brunt of sinful actions directed toward them from other people.

The second part of the forgiveness petition illuminates the connectedness of inner forgiveness and outer behavior as a result of that forgiveness. It is highly significant that Jesus places this ethical demand upon us as disciples in the setting of our own experience of forgiveness and the grace that accompanies it.

In this part of the prayer we have the classic portrayal of what theologians describe as "evangelical ethics" or what Dietrich Bonhoeffer called "formation ethics." It is the ethical mandate that emerges out of fullness rather than from scolding demands or the grief of guilt. To put it plainly—we are first forgiven by God, and then we are commanded to express that same forgiveness toward those around us. It isn't that we invent forgiveness from within our own resources but that we share the forgiveness we have already received.

Martin Luther added more to our understanding of this prayer–petition when he said, "See, this is the twofold forgiveness; one internal in the heart, that clings alone in the word of God; and one external, that breaks forth and assures us that we have the internal one." Now we see that when we forgive other people, by this very act we have the positive assurance that our own forgiveness by Jesus Christ is real. In other words, we have exercised grace when we have forgiven and have found it more than sufficient. Therefore, even in the commands of Jesus we find the good news of Jesus. Practically this means that if we want to be more certain of God's love for us personally and uniquely, we should risk sharing God's love with others more often, and in so doing we would see just how real that love is.

The Lord of the Prayer

I believe Dr. W. D. Davies suggested that the words of the Sermon on the Mount will lead us ultimately to the One who spoke them. In terms of this particular prayer–petition, when we meet the Lord who spoke these words and who taught this prayer, we meet the One who makes forgiveness possible, because Jesus himself fulfilled the prayer. In following this line of thought, we see that forgiveness is possible because of the identification of Jesus Christ with us—without him there would be no forgiveness. Each of the requests in the Lord's Prayer reaches out toward the kingly reign of Christ, and this request—"Forgive us our debts"—also reaches out for resolution of a complicated moral and spiritual crisis in our lives by the Lord of the kingdom himself.

So tightly interconnected is the crisis of human sinfulness with who we are and what we fear, the desires that motivate life, and the real harm that we have become involved in that the resolution of such a crisis takes the total help of the One who created us. The prayer for forgiveness asks for that total help, because the power of that help is so profoundly far-reaching that it is understandable how this request should break out from the forgiveness we have received and be expressed by us toward those around us.

God Is for Us!

Swiss theologian Karl Barth spoke of forgiveness as the power of powers—"the discovery that God is for me." The personal experience of forgiveness is so radical that it alters everything—my understanding of other people, my behavior, and the way I know myself. Like a great banner of peace, forgiveness signals a new chance for hope in that ancient battleground of the soul. It brings God's peace into that soul at war, with the healing balm of God's wondrous gift of a new beginning.

Jesus' marvelous story of the Prodigal Son gives us a profoundly moving example of forgiveness. In what some have called the greatest short story ever written, our Lord tells of a wayward son who breaks his father's heart by demanding his inheritance, leaving home, and becoming involved in a sinful way of life. Finally, things become so bad that he becomes desperate, " '. . . How many of my father's hired hands have bread enough and to spare, but here I am dying of hunger! I will get up and go to my father, and I will say to him, "Father, I have sinned against heaven and before you; I am no longer worthy to be called your son; treat me like one of your hired hands" ' " (Luke 15:17–19).

But the forgiving father would have none of that. Instead, he dressed the returning son in a new robe and put a ring on his finger, killed the fatted calf and threw a party—a grand celebration (15:20–24).

By contrast, James Oglethorpe (1696–1785), the stern and exacting British general and founder of the colony of Georgia, once said to John Wesley, "I never forgive." Wesley's reply was classic, "Then I hope, Sir, that you never sin!"

The poor general is like the lonely elder brother in the Prodigal Son story, who, when he heard the celebration noise from his wayward brother's party " 'became angry and refused to go in' " because he wouldn't forgive. Such self-righteous arrogance! But again, the loving father went out to find the older son and said, " ' "Son, you are always with me, and all that is mine is yours" ' " (15:25–32). With those gracious words the father invited his self-righteous and lonely older son to agree with him about forgiveness. This meant that the father himself had to bear the alienation of both the younger and the elder son—such is the costly mystery behind this forgiveness that Jesus invites us to discover as we pray, " '. . . Forgive us our debts. . . .' "

13

Total Help for Total Need

In both the Gospels of Matthew and Luke the Lord's Prayer ends with one final request, " 'And do not bring us to the time of trial, but rescue us from the evil one' " (Matthew 6:13). The familiar King James translation of this reads, "And lead us not into temptation. . . ," and other translations have it, "Do not put us to the test. . . ." The Greek word for "temptation," "test," or "time of trial" is *peirao;* another comparable English word for it would be "peril." In other words, "Lead us not into perils too great for us to bear, and protect us from the evil one."

The word "temptation" is a fierce and frightening one in both English and in the language of the Bible. *Peirao* means to destroy by degrees, to place someone under the peril of intense, gradual stress. In some cases, it may mean "to test," in a positive sense. But such usage does not lessen the frightening aspect of *peirao,* when it appears in a hostile context. In those instances translators use the English word "tempt" or "temptation."

To understand what the Scriptures mean, we need to look closely at the context in which *peirao* appears. Does it intend and imply healthy testing that moves the Christian toward maturity and hope or destructive temptation, leading to despair and loss of hope? If it implies destructive temptation, a devious and deceptive quality is always contextually attached to the word. When used in a positive sense, the word is a logical part of a discipleship experience and growth. Usually, though, in life situations we find it hard to know at first just what kind of testing we are experiencing.

The Peril of Temptation

Temptation's peril is quite different from the peril we experience from an outright frontal attack by an announced adversary. Temptation produces a much more subtle stress, because it encourages its victims to act in a self-destructive way.

A vivid illustration of the peril of temptation appears in the book *A Separate Peace,* by John Knowles. As an initiation stunt, older boys force some younger, less physically strong ones to jump from a high, overhanging tree into a river. The jump is designed to place stress on the younger boys, especially one particular boy; it is way beyond their athletic competence. Because of this, the jump is not a contest as such but a temptation—the goal is not to test skill but to incite fear and harm. The younger boys risk the jump simply because they desire to please and be accepted by those they mistakenly thought were their friends.

This is temptation in the rawest sense. To the unsophisticated onlooker it may appear the tempted person is purposely involved in a self-destructive act. But in reality a tempter has lured that person into a bad choice or decision. In most instances temptation doesn't aim to cause physical harm, but has as its goal psychological and spiritual entrapment. For example, a person may ask another a tempting question, not because he or she desires an answer, but to deceive the other—indicating a hostile intent.

Spiritual Conditioning

We can only know whether *peirao* is used in the hostile sense or in the positive sense if we carefully examine the motivational context of each usage. In the positive sense, the stressful experience purposes to strengthen our lives. For example, the rigorous conditioning a football coach puts his team through prepares them for an opening game. The coach's goal is not to harm the players but to condition them so they can handle the physical and emotional stresses of the game.

This lay behind Jesus' seemingly impossible instructions to his disciples to provide food for the huge crowd that had stayed with them for so long. When the disciples suggested to Jesus that he should send the people home, because they were hungry, he replied, " 'They need not go away; you give them something to eat' " (Matthew 14:16). Now, Jesus didn't make the impossible suggestion that his disciples provide food for five thousand people to embarrass and discredit them. He did it to strengthen them, so they would be better able to meet the challenges of the future.

This particular event is recorded in each of the four Gospels. In telling the story, the Gospel of John words it: "When he looked up and saw a large crowd coming toward him, Jesus said to Philip, 'Where are we to buy bread for these people to eat?' He said this to *test* [*peirao*] him, for he himself knew what he was going to do" (John 6:5, 6, *italics mine*). Philip immediately answered that six months' wages wouldn't be enough money. But John continues, ". . . One of his disciples, Andrew, Simon Peter's brother, said to him, 'There is a boy here who has five barley loaves and two fish. But what are they among so many people?' " (John 6:7–9).

At that point Jesus took the boy's lunch and blessed it; the entire crowd was fed, and the leftovers filled twelve baskets. What an awesome display of Jesus' power! This "test" didn't harm or make the disciples fearful; instead, they were permanently strengthened. Jesus, like a good football coach, put his team under a healthy stress in order to make them stronger and make them learn more about who Jesus really is.

Temptation's Hidden Agenda

Temptation is altogether different. It uses stress to demoralize the tempted person or persons. Outside, the "temptation stress" and the "test" stress may appear the same, but temptation's motives, whether subtle or blatant, have one purpose—to cause harm and destruction. The hidden agenda becomes clear: According to the Bible, temptation is always evil. James makes this abundantly clear, "No one when tempted, should say, 'I am being tempted by God'; for God cannot be tempted by evil and he himself tempts no one. But one is tempted by one's own desire, being lured and enticed by it; then when that desire has conceived, it gives birth to sin, and when it is fully grown, gives birth to death. Do not be deceived, my beloved" (James 1:13–16). Indeed, God doesn't test us in order to break us. Instead, like a good coach, he disciplines us to build us up for the endurance of the game of life.

The devil tempts. In fact, he is called the tempter (Matthew 4:3). This means that if for any reason we play out that destructive role toward other people or toward any part of God's creation, we have assumed the strategy of the evil one. Any question or statement intended to harm another person is an act of temptation, regardless of how pure or innocent the outward appearance. It originates in hell, and God will judge it for what it is, not by how it appears.

Such evil is at the core of such public or private events as bullfights, cockfights, or pit-bull fights. In each case, under the masquerade of "sport," persons have created a disruptive setting, a cruel hoax, into which they place these animals. After fatally tempting the animals, human participants and spectators—the tempters—watch them respond in panic. These creatures are a part of God's good creation, and we as humans have been entrusted by God to be their stewards. I firmly believe that just as God will judge us for sin against other people, he will judge us for these "games" of terror.

It is important that we understand the two kinds of stress, because some human stress experiences are harmful, while others are healthy. We need to understand the all-important differences between the healthy conviction of the Holy Spirit and the temptation of the devil. For example, if a line of questioning or an experience leads me to conclude that I am not only sinful but without hope, the Holy Spirit has not convicted me of sin. Instead, the evil one has tempted me, encouraging me to distrust God's love and faithfulness.

The conviction of sin by the Holy Spirit always leads toward the Redeemer, toward hope. Repentance and redemption are the end results of the work of the Holy Spirit; the stress the spirit of God puts upon us works in our favor.

Temptation may also stimulate a way of thinking that leads away from God. I may be tempted to feel personally righteous and without any need of forgiveness or grace. But this results in lonely isolation. I may be tempted to despair. Each of these is the work of the temptation of evil. Both lead toward aloneness, loss of freedom, and distrust in the faithfulness of God. In the one case, I don't think I need God because of a false perception of my greatness. In the other, I'm afraid to need God, because I accept the false idea that my own sinfulness placed my life outside his keeping care.

Free to Choose. Jesus Christ, the One who endured temptation, now teaches us to pray, " 'And do not bring us to the time of trial [lead us not into temptation].' " Clearly with these words Jesus encourages us to pray that we be spared the deceptive stresses that are too great for us to handle. In truth, Jesus encourages his disciples to request help from God against every subtle attack of temptation.

The prayer realistically assesses the existence of temptation's threats. Each of us can tell stories about their peril. God has granted us the ability to make choices, and the tempter tries to destroy that freedom by leading us to use it badly. Because our Lord does not rob us of freedom in our discipleship journey, temptation remains a real possibility at every point along the way.

The good news is that we know Jesus Christ himself stands with us in the face of every temptation, and he understands every danger posed to us by temptation. Even more, Jesus has invited his disciples—including us—to ask help from the Father in combating temptation of any and every kind.

The Origin of Temptation

The parallel request, " '. . . but rescue us from the evil one,' " reminds us that the origin of temptation is Satan. Consequently, this prayer–petition bears witness to our complex and real freedom. Temptation is our problem because we have the privilege and responsibility that enables us to make decisions on major matters. For example, a tree isn't tempted to choose against good soil; a cat isn't tempted when a bird is exposed to its leap, because the cat is unaware of the bird's rights and dignity. Only human beings make such value decisions. The dramatic freedom that God has given to us carries with it the real problems of choice.

Christian Warfare

The biblical writers take evil's existence seriously, not only in the sense of human failure, but also in the larger context of this prayer–petition. The biblical witness makes it clear that God, in his sovereign wisdom, has provided for human freedom so that we are able to choose *against* his good will for us. In the same way Scripture affirms God has allowed a freedom that results in the existence of evil at the spiritual level of reality. The Scripture treats with complete seriousness the existence of this greater evil called the devil, Satan, Apollyon, the tempter, and the evil one.

Saint John Chrysostom (A.D. 347?–407), an early church father and patriarch of Constantinople, stated that in praying, ". . . rescue us from the evil one," we signal once and for all that we are engaged as Christians in a battle against all forms of evil—a battle that knows no truce. In this battle we need God's resources, because behind all evil is "the evil one." This means that there are many different kinds of evil—there are bad choices made by human beings and the wider crisis of dehumanization in the social realm, but behind it all lies evil at the cosmic or spiritual level of creation.

Evil at the spiritual-heavenly level of creation poses a profound mystery for us. But the Bible describes this cosmic evil in terms of the evil one, Satan, the devil who stands in opposition to the will and purposes of God at the cosmic level of the created order. In this prayer–petition, Jesus gives us the description of the one who decided to pit his will against the will of God as "the evil one."

From the point of view of the Bible we will not have realistically grappled with human evil and earthly wickedness unless we have also wrestled this "will against God's will" at the cosmic level of creation. In other words, the battle against evil involves more than our own individual struggles.

This multidimensional nature of the problem of evil has been attested to not only in the Bible but in most great literature and especially in the long history of folk stories, ancient myths, and fantasy literature. In these, evil is rarely portrayed as simple or one dimensional, as anyone familiar with such stories as *Snow White and the Seven Dwarfs, The Wizard of Oz, Grimm's Fairy Tales,* The Chronicles of Narnia and J. R. R. Tolkien's The Lord of the Rings will recognize. In each of these the writers have woven into their stories the different kinds and forms of the threats of evil encountered by their villains and heroes. These stories enable us to see parallels to the dangers and threats we face in our own lives.

Among the most successful motion pictures of the last ten or fifteen years are three adventure movies by George Lucas—*Star Wars, The Empire Strikes Back,* and *Return of the Jedi*—all adventure stories portrayed in a modern, space-technology motif. Though other story motifs of good and evil found in Eastern religious thought are present, nevertheless, the essential story line and the portrayals of the contest between good and evil within each of these films are very much in the tradition of the folk sagas of Europe, Iceland, and ancient Greece.

We find in these classic motion pictures the evil of faceless soldiers who only follow orders in blind obedience. We discover, too, the evil of weakness shown by those who refuse to take risks and stand up for truth—truth that is repressed because of their fears. Pictured, too, are the evils perpetrated by terrorizing thugs and bullies, self-indulgence, and bureaucratic lust.

More deadly, however, are those forms of spiritual evil in which we confront wickedness that was once allied with truth, but like a fallen angel of light has betrayed all that is right. This form of evil seeks the destruction of what once it held in friendship and loyalty. Spiritual evil is more generic and radical than the violence of the ruthless marauders or the sexual chaos of Sodom and Gomorrah.

George Lucas in his movies, like J. R. R. Tolkien in his books has portrayed for us in fictional terms the large-scale battle between good and evil. These are exciting stories because of their element of adventure, but they are also exciting at another level because they are part of a larger body of folk stories that point to our human awareness of the continuing contest between good and evil. At the same time they lay open the truth of our consciousness that behind all kinds of human and interpersonal harm is the cosmic reality of evil best described as their moral, personal, spiritual will against the ultimate good will of God.

Seventeenth-century Puritan Thomas Watson expressed it well in some of his comments on the Lord's Prayer, "Satan envies man's happiness. To see a clod of dust so near to God, and himself, once a glorious angel, cast out of heavenly paradise, makes him pursue mankind with inveterate hatred."

The Victory Is Won

The devil has a measure of power, but not the final power. In the Lord's Prayer, Jesus gives us great good news: He has intervened on our behalf. God has set a boundary limiting the full extent of every evil power's terror, and we need to recognize that boundary. As we pray the words of the prayer Jesus gave to the disciples, that, too, becomes part of the boundary.

Speaking of the devil, the writer of the Book of Revelation refers to him as "the angel of the bottomless pit; his name in Hebrew is Abaddon, and in Greek he is called Apollyon" (Revelation 9:11). The word *Apollyon* means "destroyer." While Satan calls himself that, it becomes clear that he does not have the power he claims to have.

Though the evil one has the power to accuse, slander, and tempt—and we find all these names of the devil in the Bible—he does not have the power to ultimately destroy.

In John Bunyan's classic, *Pilgrim's Progress,* in his great battle with Apollyon, Pilgrim discovers that beyond all harm that evil can do there is a boundary that belongs to Jesus Christ, Lord of redemption and final victor over the evil one. Jesus Christ has the real and lasting power, and from him we receive the spiritual weapons that will conquer cosmic evil. Consequently, from the standpoint of New Testament teaching, it is extremely important that we not overrate the powers of spiritual evil.

The power of this brief and crystal-clear petition in the Lord's Prayer rests in its ability to set us free from any fear of the evil one. We need only this prayer sentence to win out in the practical give-and-take of life over any and all forms of evil. In fact, it is important that we avoid any exaggeration of the power of evil.

When we find ourselves guilty of overestimating the power of evil forces, we must remember that such an attitude or outlook represents a shrinkage of our confidence in the faithfulness and authority of Jesus Christ. I have known good Christian folk who seemed almost resigned to the notion that sin and evil would prevail and take over in our world. But this is wrong, and giving in to such an attitude in reality means we surrender our responsibility for our decisions and acts.

It is never correct to give in to the idea that "the devil made me do it." The devil only tempts; we decide and act. Therefore we must repent and ask for forgiveness, must seek God's help as we ask, and thank God for his goodness and faithfulness.

We are engaged in a larger battle than the simple contest between our own selfishness and the good will of God. How can we hope to win this cosmic battle? Only through the help of the One who fully understands each strategy of the battle. He who made this prayer possible—its author and our teacher—makes us able to win, for he has won the battle through his cross and the empty grave. His victory fulfills this prayer–petition. In the face of the evil one, we place our confidence in the truth that Jesus Christ has the upper hand.

With this truth fixed firmly in our hearts and minds, we need not become preoccupied with the evil one. Instead, it is God's perfect will for us to simply pray when either threats or danger confronts us. He has already rescued us from the evil one—our task is to trust the victory.

14

Kingdom, Power, and Glory

As we near the completion of our examination of the Lord's Prayer we come to the final sentence, ". . . For thine is the kingdom, and the power, and the glory, for ever. Amen" (Matthew 6:13 KJV).

In most instances this sentence is not found in later translations of the prayer. If included, it appears in either parentheses or brackets. The sentence is not found in the most ancient manuscripts, therefore many interpreters conclude that early Christians added it in a reverent attempt to round out the otherwise abrupt ending.

Two Options

I include the sentence because we are familiar with it, and because it does appear in several early manuscripts.

We'll approach this problem by giving consideration to two ideas. First, if we omit the final sentence, it means our Lord has given us a prayer that is like a door opening into a larger room. With this brief prayer he has taught us how to enter into that larger room. Now that we have entered that room where our Father is, we can bring ourselves and our needs and our feelings to him. We are free to "blurt" them out, because we know that he hears and cares. Entering into this room enables us to enter into the fellowship of worship, praise, and intercession that the Lord's Prayer makes possible. Jesus has taught us a prayer with which to begin our own prayers, which move us on in our intimate relationship with God. If we do not include this line, the prayer stops without an ending—not even an Amen.

But what if this final sentence does in fact belong in the prayer, since certain old manuscripts include it? The second-century document *The Didache* contains this final sentence. Professor W. D. Davies, a noted Bible scholar, is convinced that this sentence is an essential part of Jesus' prayer and belongs in the text: "It is antecedently unlikely that Matthew and, for that matter, Jesus Himself should finish a prayer without a doxology, expressed or assumed . . . secondly, (according to Pharisee tradition) every benediction had to be responded to with the full doxology . . . 'praised be His name whose glorious Kingdom is forever and ever.' "[1] As interpreters, the dilemma we must face is the fact that this final sentence is missing from the most valuable and oldest manuscripts of the New Testament.

Further, if Jesus had given his followers a prayer without the usual ending, it is quite understandable that early church scribes might seek to fulfill Old Testament tradition and first-century Jewish worship practices by supplying a doxology. In any case, note that this final sentence is identical in theme to the benedictions found in two of David's prayers. The Chronicles writer says:

> Then David blessed the Lord in the presence of all the assembly; David said: "Blessed are you, O Lord, the God of our ancestor Israel, forever and ever. Yours, O Lord, are the greatness, the power, the glory, the victory, and the majesty; for all that is in the heavens and on earth is yours; yours is the kingdom, O Lord, and you are exalted as head above all. Riches and honor come from you, and you rule over all. In your hand are power and might; and it is in your hand to make great and to give strength to all. And now, our God, we give thanks to you and praise your glorious name."
>
> 1 Chronicles 29:10–13

Similar wording is found also in David's benediction recorded in 1 Chronicles 16:36. The opening sentences of Jesus' high priestly prayer, found in chapter 17 of the Gospel of John, form another interesting parallel to the doxology that concludes the Lord's Prayer.

"Thine Is the Kingdom." Let's take a closer look at the doxology ending to the Lord's Prayer. In this magnificent shout of praise we find three facts about God's character. The first is related to the phrase, "Thine is the kingdom" (KJV). "Kingdom" was a highly charged word in the first century. Jesus picked up on the kingdom reference in the very first sentence of the Sermon on the Mount, " 'Blessed are the poor in spirit, for theirs is the kingdom of heaven' " (Matthew 5:3). The nine beatitudes that introduce the sermon make it clear that Jesus is revealing a new and deeper definition of kingdom. Because of their confinement within the narrow limitations of tribalism and nationalistic aspiration, the disciples of Jesus would only gradually discover the meaning of "kingdom" as Jesus used it.

For Jesus, the kingdom of heaven or the kingdom of God was a reference to "kingly reign"—the relationship between God and his people. The disciples would only begin to understand the meaning of the kingdom as they experienced the catastrophic event of Jesus' death on Calvary and the glorious victory, three days later, on that first Easter morning, when Jesus conquered sin and death through his resurrection. In time they would understand that the meaning of the kingdom is defined by the King himself. The kingdom is where the King is, and those who follow the King are in the kingdom.

By the time of the first church council held in Jerusalem, the first-century believers had reached agreement on the fact that God's kingdom is universally available to everyone who has faith—Jews and gentiles—to all who trust in Jesus Christ. This cataclysmic decision for the Jewish believers of Jerusalem resulted from Peter's experience with Cornelius and the testimony of Barnabas and Paul as they reported gentile conversions.

James, the chairperson for that first council, quoted from the Book of the Twelve—the Minor Prophets—to validate the council's decision. Quoting from the Greek version of the Prophet Amos (Amos 9:8–12), James says, " 'After this I will return, and I will rebuild the dwelling of David, which has fallen; from its ruins I will rebuild it, and I will set it up, so that all other people may seek the Lord—even all the Gentiles over whom my name has been called. Thus says the Lord, who has been making these things known from long ago' " (Acts 15:16, 17).

This is the kingdom of God for which we praise him—it

is the kingly reign that belongs to God and becomes the gift to every believer. To this kingdom and this King we sing the praise of this last sentence of our Lord's Prayer.

"And the power." Here, we offer thanks to God for his power and his authority. According to the New Testament teaching, the Christian finds power in the confidence that God is a God of power. As believers we cannot control or make use of power in pursuing our purposes and goals. The good news of the gospel is found in the assurance of the authority that resides with the Son of God. Because Jesus Christ has that authority, it means that no other force—human evil, death, angels, the devil—has that power. Rather, all power centers in Christ and in his reign—all of history is bounded by the love of Christ.

Having established this eternal truth, we also conclude that a tremendous authority comes to the believer who is assured of God's authority. It means that the believer is set free from the false powers and from paniclike fear in the face of threats of wrongful power. We see something like this in the character Jean Valjean, in Victor Hugo's *Les Misérables*.

In this moving story, Jean Valjean has experienced the tender and strong love of the priest, Father Bienvenue, in the midst of his darkest hour. The remarkable musical portrayal of this Victor Hugo classic weaves together into an impressive musical tapestry the different kinds of powers that drive men and women. It includes the surging force and power of angry people determined to destroy injustice and the power of narrow and confused righteousness in the words and actions of Javaier, the police inspector.

Then we see the power of the underground scavenger–thieves who live solely for themselves—those who cash in on the outcome of the tragedies of better people. But the greatest power of all is the power that can heal and forgive—the power that can give life in the place of death. Jean Valjean experienced this love from Jesus through the priest. This power of love finally transforms the powerful song of the angry and fearful men, which concludes the first act of the musical, into the song of hope that becomes the final melody of the closing scene.

Jesus has done this very same thing with the Jewish language of the kingdom. He has transformed the fierce songs of the kingdom that were so common to the people in the first century. In the Qumran community, on the shores of the Dead Sea, archaeological discoveries have produced parchments containing the harsh, nationalistic songs of a people protesting outside rule, oppression, and authority. Jesus transformed the militant kingdom yearnings of the nationalist zealots into the universal song of hope for all people who are conquered not by violence but by love.

This is authentic power: It is worth having, and we receive it from Jesus Christ once we are assured of his forgiveness and his victory over death. This is not the power one person has over another.

We need this power of love most. Unlike all other powers, it never corrupts those who receive it. Its grace "buys our souls for God."

"And the glory." In both the Old and New Testaments glory has to do with the presence of God. Because of the awareness of "presence" in the word, a sense of luminosity and spectacle accompanies the biblical portrayals of glory. The dramatic encounter between the Prophet Isaiah and the Lord vividly shows this. With color and imagery, the prophet says,

> In the year that King Uzziah died, I saw the Lord sitting on a throne, high and lofty; and the hem of his robe filled the temple. Seraphs were in attendance above him; each had six wings; with two they covered their faces, and with two they covered their feet, and with two they flew. And one called to another and said: "Holy, holy, holy is the Lord of hosts; *the whole earth is full of his glory."*
>
> Isaiah 6:1–3, *italics mine*

Matthew captures this same mystery and glory as he describes the scene on the Mount of Transfiguration, "Six days later, Jesus took with him Peter and James and his brother John and led them up a high mountain, by themselves. *And he was transfigured before them, and his face shown like the sun, and his clothes became dazzling white"* (Matthew 17:1, 2, *italics mine*).

In the Book of Revelation's colorful imagery, we catch a marvelous picture of the glory of God the Father and the Lamb in the majestic words of the song:

> ". . . Holy, holy, holy, the Lord God the Almighty, who was and is and is to come." And whenever the living creatures gave glory and honor and thanks to the one who is seated on the throne, who lives forever and ever, the twenty-four elders fall before the one who is seated on the throne and worship the one who lives forever and ever; they cast their crowns before the throne, singing, "You are worthy, our Lord and God, *to receive glory and honor and power,* for you created all things, and by your will they existed and were created."
>
> Revelation 4:8–11, *italics mine*

The word "glory" carries within its meanings the sense of our recognition of ultimate worth. We sing the *Gloria* in Christian worship when we have discovered the worthiness of God. This is why the *Gloria* follows great affirmations about God.

Only God deserves a word as large as *Glory!* And it is his to share that glory as he chooses with humanity. When a human being has caught the vision of the disclosure of the character of God by the Lord himself, then the word *glory* becomes appropriate as the best description he can come up with through the use of the inadequate human vocabulary.

The word "glory," as used throughout the Old and New Testaments, signals to us that God deserves our praise. When God himself draws us into his presence, as new men and women we may share in his glory in a reflected way. Paul's majestic and affirmative words to the Christians at Rome describe this:

> We know that all things work together for good for those who love God, who are called according to his purpose. For those whom he foreknew he also predestined to be conformed to the image of his Son, in order that he might be the firstborn within a large family. And those whom he predestined he also called; and those whom he called he also justified; *and those whom he justified he also glorified.*
>
> Romans 8:28–30, *italics mine*

We experience God's great decision in our favor through approval of us—what the Apostle Paul refers to as the "weight of glory" (2 Corinthians 4:17). But for us, glory is a complicated experience, because we experience its "weight." But we can accept the fact with confidence that the glory of Jesus Christ does shine upon us and that weight of his presence is a gift granted to us just as we received the gift of his gracious forgiveness.

C. S. Lewis explored the meanings of that "weight of glory" in a sermon he preached to Oxford students in 1939. Among other things he said,

> . . . Either glory means to me fame, or it means luminosity . . . the desire for fame appears to me as a competitive passion and therefore of hell rather than heaven. As for the second, who wishes to become kind of a living electric light bulb? When I began to look into this matter I was shocked to find such different Christians as Milton, Johnson, and Thomas Aquinas taking heavenly glory quite frankly in the sense of fame or good report. But not fame conferred by our fellow creatures—fame with God, approval or (I might say) "appreciation" by God. And then when I had thought it over, I saw that this view was scriptural; nothing can eliminate from the parable in the divine accolade, "Well done, thou good and faithful servant." With that, a good deal of what I had been thinking all my life fell down like a house of cards. I suddenly remembered that nothing is so obvious in a child—not in a conceited child, but in a good child—as its great and undisguised pleasure in being praised.[2]

There is no more vital experience than to know the King and his sovereign righteousness, knowing his ultimate worthiness and then experiencing his approval. Can you see now how this final doxology in the Lord's Prayer has brought us full circle to the opening four commandments that God gave to Moses on Mount Sinai? We have been brought to the great "worship commandments," and these point us toward God and his character. In this magnificent doxology we have the best protection against idolatry, vanity, polytheism, and meaninglessness. When we really know the King—who he is and his authority and worthiness—we no longer need the idols of Baal, the Roman city gods, or any of the false gods of our late twentieth century. The doxology that closes out the Lord's Prayer turns our eyes upon the Lord himself.

For Ever. Amen. This brings us now to the closing words, "For ever. Amen" (KJV). Here we have the words of fulfillment and faithfulness. "For ever" is not used in the Greek sense of infinity. Rather, it is used in the Hebrew sense of completion, and this is affirmed to us by its companion word "Amen"—a word brought directly into the Greek from Hebrew.

"Amen" in its concrete Hebrew sense and meaning is defined as "foundation stone" or "pillar," as, for example, in 2 Kings 18:16, where it is used to describe the doorposts of the Temple. In Isaiah 22:23 the word "Amen" is translated "peg in a secure place." And the same word is used in a double form at the close of Psalm 41:13, where it is "Amen and Amen." In this instance it means the faithfulness of God, followed by the response of our faith. This is probably the intention of our Lord's double use of the word at the opening of many of his speeches. For example, it is this word Jesus used when he said, " 'Very truly [Amen, amen] I tell you . . .' " (John 1:51). Over and over again in the Gospel of John especially we have the words, "Verily, verily" or "truly, truly." In each case, the original is "Amen, amen." God's faithfulness for our faith.

In this doxology, as throughout the Lord's Prayer, we have the sense of the awesome majesty and holiness of God, but at the same time we feel the presence of a loving heavenly Father who cares for us, provides for us, and is at all times intimately aware of our feelings and needs. Indeed, through our prayer we feel the intimacy of friendship with the One who is described in these words, "And the Word became flesh and lived among us, and we have seen his glory, the glory as of a father's only son, full of grace and truth" (John 1:14).

15

Daily Prayer

Christians not only require daily bread, we also need daily prayer. Saint Augustine explained the reason for this need when he wrote in his *Confessions:* "Our hearts are restless until they find their rest in Thee." Prayer is a rest in the Lord who is our Friend, because by prayer we trust and put our weight down upon the faithfulness of God.

Saint Augustine also understood the dynamic nature of prayer when he himself prayed, "But thou, Lord, ever workest, and art ever at rest . . . so rest in us as now thou workest in us." Prayer is work because in prayer we think things through with God, and we bring our real lives into the living presence of the Lord in order to hear his will and his mandate. That can hardly be a passive experience!

A Daily Rule

At this point in our prayer pilgrimage let us look at some of the ways that Christians pray. I believe that the daily rule for prayer is important, not as the requirement of a technique or a law, but because every relationship needs the continuity of communication in order to grow and deepen. For this reason, regular, daily prayer has been, and is, my goal.

I like to stand at the front window of our house and pray for the people and events that are a part of my day. Before the rest of the family is awake and up, I set apart this special time with God. When I drive to work at certain streets and one large traffic circle I sing songs of praise to God for the day. Among my favorites are, "Let the First Song I Sing Today Be Praise to You," and, "Make Me Like You, Lord, Please Make Me Like You." I'm also very fond of "O God, Our Help in Ages Past," "When I Survey the Wondrous Cross," "Amazing Grace," and "Praise the Savior Ye Who Know Him." In other words I have found it helpful to have certain habits of prayer and praise that accompany the ordinary routines of my day, including specific places that are a part of that routine. In this way, traditions become a part of my personal life journey.

It has also long been a practice in our home to pray at meal times. Part of our family tradition is to hold hands around the table as we pray.

At night we pray for a good sleep and for safety for all of our loved ones and friends. My daughter Anne and I are both journal keepers. Here we write about the people and activities in our lives. These become a very important part of our prayers as we remember the people and events recorded there.

A Structured Time and Place. I find that a daily quiet time of prayer and meditation is very important to many people, and I have attempted to build this into my own schedule. My father has structured a quiet time into each morning immediately following his regimen of body exercises. Other of my friends listen to tapes, meditate, pray, and even sing during their daily routines of jogging or walking. Another friend drives the fifty to seventy-five miles from Berkeley to Sacramento and back almost every day, and he has set aside a part of the trip each day as his time of reflection and prayer.

However, whenever we do it, each of us needs to establish our own routines and traditions that build our relationship and friendship with the Lord. C. S. Lewis commented, "Active habits are strengthened through repetition." We need active habits especially when it comes to the development of our habits of prayer.

Personal but Not Private. Ronald Thompson, a good friend of mine, commented, "Christian faith is personal but it is not private." How true! Yes, at times we want to be alone, but as Christians we have built into our biblical faith a tradition of warm and nourishing fellowship. Indeed, the Lord has called us into a relationship with himself, but he also calls us into fellowship with other people.

In fact, in the Bible's first description of Christian believers Luke wrote in the Book of Acts: "So those who welcomed his [Peter's] message were baptized. . . . They devoted themselves to the apostles' teaching and fellowship, to the breaking of bread and the prayers" (2:41, 42).

I believe that group prayer forms a vital part of the Christian's whole prayer experience. The prayer groups I have belonged to in my own Christian journey have played a key role in my spiritual formation. As a Christian I have always needed brothers and sisters who are my prayer partners.

I recall so vividly the first prayer group in which I took part. It was a college group at the First Presbyterian Church of Berkeley, and we met regularly to pray for one another and our common lives as students at the University of California. A fellow student and friend, Larry Cardwell, still stands out in my memory because of his strong faith in God. I knew that Larry was fiercely honest about everything, and when he shared with our group that he trusted God completely, it carried a lot of weight with me.

When I entered Princeton Theological Seminary, I joined a group that became very formative in my life. University and seminary students met early in the morning once a week. Whimsically, we called ourselves "the Original Twelve." We studied the Bible and prayed together. From this fellowship group I learned about the exciting power of the Bible to be relevant to our everyday life, if we are willing to be open and receptive to the text. Second, I discovered the warm and supportive fellowship that comes when we pray together with fellow Christians, and that fellowship of prayer has continued on with lifelong friends that I made in that group.

Later, during the two summers that I was a seminary intern at the First Presbyterian Church of Berkeley I learned the good discipline of a daily early-morning group that was led by Dr. Ralph Byron, a layman of the church. Our group prayed for world needs, for the ministry of missionaries and Christian workers, and for one another. In this experience of persistent intercession, I was stretched by my exposure to what Christians in other worshiping traditions have called the daily office of prayer.

The prayer-group experiences I had at Forest Home Christian Conference Center, in the San Bernardino Mountains, near Los Angeles, during the time of Dr. Henrietta Mears, especially encouraged me during the earliest years of my ministry as a pastor to students. Miss Mears had the gift of contagious, enthusiastic confidence in the power of the gospel of Jesus Christ, because she knew the Lord of that gospel so well. I recall one time when someone asked Miss Mears, who was then in her senior years, what she would do differently if she could relive her life. Without a moment of hesitation, she answered, "I would trust God more." Hers were always prayers of trust, in which she realistically took note of the problems but always kept her eyes on the Lord.

In these few paragraphs I have shared only a few experiences and people who have enriched my life because we prayed together. Dr. Robert Boyd Munger also taught me to pray; he was not only my senior colleague but my prayer colleague as well.

The Supportive Power of Shared Prayer

Today I benefit from two regular groups that play a highly significant role in my present journey as a Christian. The first group has met together every Wednesday morning, for nineteen years. We eat together, share together, pray together, and study the Bible together. The special concern of this group is to pray for one another as we attempt to fulfill our varied vocational callings. The other group, comprised of pastors, meets together monthly. Our goal is to pray for one another and the ministry and outreach of each church.

Because of the richness of my own experiences and their dramatic impact on my spiritual journey, I always encourage Christians to locate a group with which they can pray and study the Bible. And if there isn't such a group available, I ask them to consider starting one. Nothing substitutes for the supportive help and strength that we give to one another. The Apostle Paul, well aware of the power of Christian prayer fellowship and support, commented to the Christians at the church in Philippi, "For I know that through your prayers and the help of the Spirit of Jesus Christ this will turn out for my deliverance" (Philippians 1:19). The Greek word translated "help" in this verse is *epichoragia*. From the root of this word we get our English words *chorus, chorale,* and *choreography*. Here the Apostle tells us that God is the master choreographer of our lives and our prayers, even of our relational connections and meetings. We decide to pray, and in our freedom we decide what to do in our human encounters. But God choreographs our prayer and our lives to the good benefit of the world around us. This is encouraging news as we look back and look forward toward the future.

We pray and we pray together because the Lord has invited us into the place of agreement, where he meets us, and we call our experience of that place prayer—the prayer between friends. We thought it was our idea to pray—and in reality it was—the mystery of it all is that when we are in that place of agreement called prayer, we discover Someone waiting there, with a fire going and even food to eat (John 21:12, 13).

16

Between Friends

Several years ago I was invited to be the retreat speaker at an InterVarsity Christian Fellowship conference at a camp in the jungle-covered mountains near the city of Cebu in the south-central Philippines. Several of the leaders and I arrived from Manila, at an agreed-upon meeting place, so we could travel together up to the camp. The camp was located high in the mountains, above a deep, tropical, river valley.

At a small airport, an InterVarsity student leader, who knew the terrain well, met us. He had written out an elaborate set of directions and had drawn a map to guide us up through the mountains to the campsite. He showed us the four-wheel-drive truck and supplemented his written directions and the map with some added warnings. It was a hazardous four-hour trip, over a rough route; he warned us to be careful crossing the river and told us where we should go if the afternoon rains had caused the river to swell so we couldn't cross at the prescribed place. Finally he warned us to watch the edges of the cliffs carefully, in case of mud slides or a possible washout.

Apparently, the looks on our faces betrayed the terror we felt down inside. After a few minutes of such descriptive instructions, he stopped and looked from one of us to another. Then came the first good news we'd heard since we arrived, "Oh, heck, I'll go with you guys, and I'll drive."

In that happy moment, which made the humid Philippine afternoon bearable, I learned a very important life principle: A guide alongside is infinitely better than a map and written instructions. And the great good news for us, in our Christian journey, is that Jesus Christ is the Guide who has joined us. He guides us, not because we have hired him or because he feels sorry for us, but because he is our Friend. We may find it difficult to understand why he wants to be our Friend and Companion, but over and over again in the Gospels we have the record that his words and actions prove his friendship.

What Is This Friendship?

In Jesus' Thursday-evening discourse during Passion Week, one paragraph in particular gives us a graphic affirmation and explanation of God's friendship with us:

> "This is my commandment, that you love one another as I have loved you. No one has greater love than this, to lay down one's life for one's friends. *You are my friends if you do what I command you.* I do not call you servants any longer, because the servant does not know what the master is doing; *but I have called you friends,* because I have made known

> to you everything that I have heard from my Father. You did not choose me but I chose you. And I appointed you to go and bear fruit, fruit that will last, so that the Father will give you whatever you ask in my name. I am giving you these commands so that you may love one another."
>
> John 15:12–17, *italics mine*

Two important questions surface here: What did it mean to the disciples to be friends of the Lord at that place and time during Holy Week? What does it mean for us today?

The First Test. In this brief New Testament paragraph Jesus offers four tests of the friendship he is describing—two tests from his side and two from our side. From Jesus' side comes the first test: We know Christ's friendship for us because of what he has done *for* us: " 'No one has greater love than this, to lay down one's life for one's friends.' "

The reasoning behind this test of friendship is that the depth and extent of self-giving love is the most fundamental and timeless criterion of friendships. We instinctively employ this criterion when we are in trouble and need help—whom can I call on the phone at one in the morning, when my car breaks down?

We all have acquaintances whom we enjoy meeting at church or at work or on the golf course or at a civic club. But we wouldn't ask a favor from most of these people, because we instinctively realize there exists an unwritten but real limitation to the degree of commitment that can be expected from these relationships. After all, they are acquaintances, not friends.

All our relationships carry different weights. We are indeed fortunate if a few people in our lives would give us the shirts off their backs. Psychologist Jess Lair words it this way, "How many close friends can you have? Two, three, four? One of my definitions of a close friend is a guy who is around when you need him. And it isn't because you called him up, he is around because he is your friend."[1]

Jesus underscored his friendship for his disciples by saying that he would give his life for them, because they were his friends. A little later he assured them, " '. . . And remember, I am with you always . . .' " (Matthew 28:20). That's the kind of Friend Jesus is. The good news for us is that he includes those of us who live twenty centuries later in that promise of friendship. The promise is definite, personal, and historical, and it became an event on Mount Calvary.

The Second Test. The second test on Jesus' side of this friendship equation is a more subtle expansion of the first. Jesus wants the disciples to understand his friendship not only in sacrificial and heroic terms but in the interpersonal framework of communication. Jesus tells his disciples that he has taken them into his confidence in a way only experienced among close and good friends, " '. . . I have made known to you everything . . .' " (John 15:15), and this proves the friendship.

Have you had a moment at a bus station or on a commuter train platform when out of the corner of your eye you caught sight of a familiar face? At such times a dilemma confronts me. I had counted on the next thirty minutes or so on that train or bus to study my notes for an upcoming lecture. If I acknowledge seeing this "friend," it could result in our sitting together, and I would lose out on my precious time of study.

Now, such an occasion reveals just how much the person I have spotted means to me. If that person is a good friend, I will walk across the platform and suggest we ride together and visit. The previously planned study time seems less important, under the circumstances. On the other hand, if the person I've caught sight of is an especially trusted friend who knows me well, I would feel free to walk up to him and say something like this: "It's great to see you, Bob. Let's sit together, but I can't talk or visit, because I have to study my notes for a lecture I'm to give later this morning." You can see the difference in the quality of each friendship.

Another illustration of this distinction surfaces once a year at Christmastime, when we receive the usual run of Christmas letters. If a letter is from a valued friend but someone I haven't been intimately close to, I may set it aside to read at my leisure. On the other hand, if a letter arrives from someone I feel especially close to, I'll set everything else aside and pour over the letter immediately, because I'm anxious to know all that has happened to this special friend.

Jesus wanted his disciples and us to know that we are this kind of special friend. He wants to talk to us and give us the good news about his heavenly Father. An intimate quality about the friendship Jesus offers us makes our relationship warm and intensely personal.

The Third Test. Now we come to the two tests of friendship from our side of the relationship. Jesus said, " 'You are my friends *if you do what I command you*' " (John 15:14, *italics mine*). When I first pondered those words, I felt a strong tinge of disappointment, because I thought Jesus had spoken what amounted to an omnibus requirement of obedience to all of his commands. I realized that obedience was certainly a part of my discipleship responsibilities, but I felt disappointed that he would insert the demand for obedience in a statement about friendship.

However as I reflected more closely on Jesus' words I saw that here he focuses our attention not on all the rules of discipleship but on the one great commandment with which he begins and ends his statement, "This is my commandment, that you love one another . . ." and "I am giving you these commands so that you may love one another" (John 15:12, 17). When I came to terms with this very simple and clear contextual sense, in which one single command of Jesus is affirmed, I saw its good and exciting connection to my friendship with him. I realized Jesus asked us to share his friendship with other people.

To illustrate: Imagine that you are on a walking tour of a grand estate, possibly in England. Your tour guide, who also happens to be a friend of the owner, shows you through the mansion room by room. Everything you see arouses your admiration—the gardens, the swimming pool, the passageways, the dining hall, and the vaulted great hall. While looking around the great hall, you comment to your guide, "What a beautiful vase on that table over there."

The guide turns and asks, "Do you really like that vase?" "Yes, I think that is the most beautiful vase I have ever seen," you reply. With that, the guide says, "Then it is yours. I know the owner of this house very well, and my friend would want you to have the vase. It's yours."

This is exactly the idea that Jesus is getting across to his disciples. In effect, he says, "You will indeed prove that you are my friend if you give away the valued possessions of my estate, and my love is the most valuable of all. When you give my love to others, you have proved our friendship."

In his interpretation of the Lord's Prayer Martin Luther had a telling comment on the petition in which Jesus teaches us to ask forgiveness for our trespasses and then says that we are to forgive those who trespass against us. Luther observed that the second part of the petition is given to us because with it the Lord lets us see that we will experience forgiveness in a definite and practical way—we are assured of our forgiveness when we are able to forgive others who have acted against us.

When we share Christ's love, we prove inwardly and outwardly that we ourselves are experiencing that love, and in the sharing we are assured that we are friends of Jesus Christ. Think of it! We prove Christ's extravagant friendship when we extravagantly give away Christ's best treasures as if there was an endless supply!

The Fourth Test. The final test of our friendship is as simple as it is direct, " '. . . the Father will give you *whatever you ask him in my name*' " (John 15:16, *italics mine*). This test of friendship on our side is a carbon copy of the second test on Jesus' side of the equation. Jesus takes us into his confidence because he considers us his friends, and now we are invited to do the same toward him. We are encouraged to take God into our confidence, and when we do, we have the right to use the name of Jesus according to our need. Here Jesus invites us to pray to the Father in his name, without embarrassment or hesitation. In so doing we prove that Jesus is both our Friend and our Lord.

In this remarkable statement the Lord invites us to pray for the concerns on our hearts with the same openness and lack of embarrassment that go with the requests and questions that we ask of a really good friend. We can do this at any time of the day or night—even at one in the morning!

Prayer becomes one more test of the durable reality of our friendship—it is the miraculously free and privileged language between friends. As believers in Jesus Christ, when we speak of prayer, we describe a friendship that has taken the whole world by surprise. It is friendship with the One who not only willingly gave us a set of directions and a map, but he decided to come along with us on our journey of life.

17

And Finally . . .

If we want to come to a clear understanding of what God is like, we should ask ourselves one simple question: "What does prayer mean to me?"

Our response to this question goes to the very heart of what we understand God to be like. Dr. George Hendry, the Charles Hodge Professor Theology at Princeton Theological Seminary, first helped me to discover this very simple doorway into the vast territory of the theology of God. He asked this question of all the young theologians at the seminary, because he knew that when we pray—if we do—we reveal what we believe about God in a more accurate way than if we just talk *about* God. Therefore this is as much a book about what we believe about God as it is about why and how we pray to God.

If God seems an impersonal force to us, then our prayers reveal that we expect an impersonal nonlistener. On the other hand, if we understand God as the One who has spoken and made himself known in Jesus Christ, our prayers will reflect a tenaciously personal theology in the way we expect a living God of love to hear us.

Prayer is not one of several possible religious acts or disciplines that devout people might become good at or well trained to do. Rather, prayer is *our part in* and *our experience of* the very heart of the whole mystery of being and of the mystery of God. Prayer is our side of the friendship we experience in our relationship with Almighty God.

In the beginning of this journey into the meanings of prayer, I told the story of Dr. Donald Grey Barnhouse and his crisp sentence, "Our prayers don't change God but they do change us." As you can see, I have disagreed with the first part of his statement, but the second part of his sentence is wonderfully true.

Prayer does change history as we become partners of God's will—at the same time, prayer changes us. By prayer we make our complete selves open to God so that we welcome his grace and righteousness into our daily lives. This happens when we dare to pray, and somehow the mystery of prayer takes on ethical and behavioral implications.

It seems to me that somehow or other, people are more intellectually thoughtful and ethically active after praying. Prayer affects and even changes our attitudes and our way of life. That great English writer of our century Malcolm Muggeridge discovered this when he visited the Sisters of Charity Mission to the dying, in Calcutta, India. At first blush Muggeridge thought these sisters and their tiny Albanian leader, Mother Teresa, spent altogether too much time in their various offices of prayer. But then he discovered that these women of prayer had far more energy and skill and grace than they could have mustered through their human resources. These missionary sisters profoundly influenced Muggeridge as he beautifully told their story in his moving book *Something Beautiful for God.*

Yes, prayer changes us, and not because we are good at it, but because of the One to whom we open our hearts and minds when we pray. In prayer we discover that God is indeed alive and present through his Son, Jesus Christ, just as was announced by the young man in a white robe at Jesus' empty tomb, " '. . . you are looking for Jesus of Nazareth, who was crucified. *He had been raised: he is not here . . .' "* (Mark 16:6, *italics mine*).

This living Lord invites us to pray, and every time we do we confess our faith in the living God, every time we pray, we risk having our lives changed. For me, the best discovery of all is that the One who meets me in prayer is my Friend, as he has been from the beginning.

In our journey together, we have seen that prayer began very early in the Bible. Hardly a psalm, an Old Testament story, or a prophetic challenge does not in some way teach us about prayer. We saw in the Job story that he was a good teacher as he boldly dared to lay his concerns and arguments before God himself. But Job, the amateur, embarrassed his religious counselor–friends, just as all genuine prayer is a religious embarrassment, because friendship needs no religious skill or rehearsed ritual—and prayer is the language of friendship. As we've all experienced, turbulence and pain exist in friendship just as joy and quietness do. But the language of that relationship, both in times of upheaval and in times of quietness, is prayer.

Finally, we confront the eternal truth that Jesus is the best teacher of prayer, because he invites us to enter his Father's house without fear, yet with profound respect and thankfulness. As we pray, we acknowledge this gratitude in the closing words, "In Jesus' name." Here is the grand secret of all time. And that secret is the Person in whose name we pray—Jesus Christ the Lord!

First-century Roman cynic and critic of Christianity Celsus was really right when he made his brilliant charge against the early Christians: "Christians have the absurd idea that God takes an interest in man."

"For thine is the kingdom, and the power, and the glory, for ever. Amen." Prayer—the language of our friendship with God—proves Celsus was right!

Source Notes

Chapter 1: Do I Dare Disturb God?

1. T. S. Eliot, "Love Song of J. Alfred Prufrock," *The Literature of England,* George K. Anderson and William E. Buckler, eds., 5th ed., Vol. 2 (Glenview, Ill.: Scott, Foresman & Co., 1968), 1732.

Chapter 3: The Language of Relationship

1. Dietrich Bonhoeffer, *Letters & Papers From Prison* (New York: Macmillan, 1972), 157.

Chapter 6: Who Is There When We Pray?

1. C. S. Lewis, *The Screwtape Letters* (New York: Macmillan, 1967), 37.

Chapter 7: The Crisis of Faith

1. Francis I. Andersen, *Job: An Introduction and Commentary* (London: Inter-Varsity Press, 1976).

2. Karl Barth, *Dogmatics in Outline* (New York: Harper & Row, Publishers, 1959), 15.

Chapter 8: Surprised by Hope

1. Harold Kushner, *When Bad Things Happen to Good People* (New York: Schocken Books, 1987).
2. Francis I. Andersen, *Job: An Introduction and Commentary* (London: Inter-Varsity Press, 1976).

Chapter 12: Forgiveness

1. C. S. Lewis, *The Magician's Nephew* (New York: Macmillan, 1986), 141.

Chapter 14: Kingdom, Power, and Glory

1. W. D. Davies, *The Setting of the Sermon on the Mount* (Cambridge: Cambridge Univ. Press, 1964), 1.
2. C. S. Lewis, *The Weight of Glory* (Grand Rapids, Mich.: Wm. B. Eerdmans Co., 1949), 8.

Chapter 16: Between Friends

1. Jess Lair, *I Ain't Well but I Sure Am Better* (Garden City, N. Y.: Doubleday & Co., 1975), 37.